GOODBYE, MURPHY'S LAW

Whatever Can Go Wrong, God Can Make Right

JUDY PACE CHRISTIE

DIMENSIONS
FOR LIVING
NASHVILLE

GOODBYE, MURPHY'S LAW
WHATEVER CAN GO WRONG, GOD CAN MAKE RIGHT

This book is printed on acid-free paper.

Library of Congress Cataloging-in-Publication Data

Christie, Judy Pace, 1956-
  Goodbye, Murphy's Law : whatever can go wrong, God can make right / Judy Pace Christie.
    p. cm.
  ISBN 978-0-687-49208-4 (pbk., : alk. paper)
  1. Providence and government of God—Christianity.   2. Spiritual life.—Christianity.   I. Title.
BT135.C46 2008
248.4--dc22

                                                                    2007037233

08 09 10 11 12 13 14 15 16 17—10 9 8 7 6 5 4 3 2 1

MANUFACTURED IN THE UNITED STATES OF AMERICA

To Paul
with love

CONTENTS

WITH GRATITUDE

*T*his book was shaped by many lessons learned along the way from my church families—particularly at Parkview Baptist Church, Suntree United Methodist Church, and Grace Community United Methodist Church. Each of these has helped me understand more about God's plan for my life, and I give thanks to the Lord for the local church.

In this season of life, I especially learn much from pastors and leaders at Grace, including Barbara, Pete, and Pam, and Pastors Rob, Sione, Ellen, Stacy, and Rich. My life has also been enriched by the "Hurry Less, Worry Less" small group at Grace, including Becky, Beth, Jodie, Randy, Missy, Karen, Cilla, Susie, Kimberly, Thomas, Anita, Sheryl, Isabelle, David, Sandra, and Jane.

Every time I sit down to write, I do so with the encouragement of many friends and family members. I thank them all, including the Baylor FunFest Friends (especially Laura K., who shared her powerful story), the Barret Girls, and the Big Ham Small Group.

Very special thanks go to Alisa Stingley and Kathie Rowell, who listened to ideas and read early drafts; Martha H. Fitzgerald, who encouraged me to learn more about the world of writing; Sandi Walton, who helped keep my business running when I checked out to write; Pat Lingenfelter, who hopped in the car and supported me during workshops and speeches; my agent, Etta Wilson; and editor, Ron Kidd.

And, as always, I thank my husband, Paul, for all he does.

INTRODUCTION

"If you follow my decrees and are careful to obey my commands, I will send you rain in its season, and the ground will yield its crops and the trees of the field their fruit.... I will grant peace in the land, and you will lie down and no one will make you afraid." Leviticus 26:3-4, 6

*T*his past summer we had rain. On the heels of summers of drought, we received a blessed daily soaking.

The results were amazing. Yards became lush and green. Trees that had struggled flourished. Plants shot up. "I finally have the grass I have dreamed of," my husband said, following three years of trying to get growth in hard clay soil.

This change reminded me that despite our best efforts, plants will not blossom without water. These plants became what they were meant to be, not shriveling up and barely existing but bursting forth.

Our lives are like that.

When we seek to know and do God's will, we can be so much more, springing forth in new ways and flourishing. We were created for special things. We are to enjoy each day and love others and find ways to serve. This journey includes hope, the water for our souls.

But often we create drought conditions for ourselves. We

live in a world where people tend to expect the worst. This is where our friend Murphy comes in. Almost all of us can recite Murphy's Law: Whatever *can* go wrong *will* go wrong. Many people act as if they live under the weight of it.

God has an amazing plan for each of us, and this plan is not some elusive, mystical riddle we cannot decipher. We can move past dry spells and give up dread and fear. We can shape a vision for our life that is large and special and meaningful.

On a recent Sunday morning at church, a line of graduating high school students stood before our congregation, taking the microphone to tell what they hoped to do with their lives. Some were absolutely certain: medicine, telecommunications. Others were a bit more cautious, including one young woman who got a laugh as she announced that she was currently majoring in "undecided." Watching these seniors, awkward and yet clearly excited, I was reminded of how life unfolds with great promise and opportunity—and how God wants to use us all along the way.

Although more than three decades have passed since I stood as part of a similar high school group, I still find myself standing before God with an awkward excitement. As the years have passed, I have sometimes been one of the certain ones—marching forward, feeling the touch of God's hand on my back. At other times—even now, firmly in middle age—I have wrestled with knowing God's will, longing for clear direction and a calm spirit.

Mix in a Monday morning here and there, and I have a concoction that does not look like the great life God has in store for me. I sometimes awaken feeling a bit overloaded. My mind starts pinging with all the to-dos, not only for that day but for the rest of the week. I am tired, wondering why I didn't get the last load of laundry done, the bills paid, the house straightened up. As I think of Murphy's Law—an outlook that says the worst is likely to happen—my heart feels restless, and I anticipate a tough week at work, knowing there will be problems to solve and fires to put out. (I sometimes think if it were not for Monday mornings and Murphy, I might be a perfect person, doing God's will much more consistently with a smile on my face.)

In my work as a consultant and workshop leader, I find that many people share these same feelings. They want to *know* what God wants them to do. They want to *do* what God wants them to do. But in the business of everyday life, they are pulled off the path and wind up longing for a calm, certain spirit.

In some ways this is a scary topic. God's will? How can I possibly know? If I have hope in a world that usually expects the worst, will I look like a fool? But it is also an exhilarating subject that can expand our lives and help us enjoy each day more. We can identify the conditions we need in order to flourish. We can learn to pray about this and to know how God is guiding us. We can become more familiar with the Bible and the words of help it provides. We can take everyday steps to move closer to being the people God wants us to be. We can change directions when we go astray and learn to move past the bad times.

Sure, we may have to learn some of these lessons more than once. And life will have its bumps and twists. We will have to learn and grow until we change our daily thoughts and decisions, and seize hope. Contentment can become a way of life. We can savor the joy that comes from knowing that God has a better plan for us.

Goodbye, Murphy's Law. We will seek a new way, a way that expects good things to happen, a way that believes God's plans for us are spectacular and that God is with us no matter what happens, good or bad.

Chapter One

THE KEY

HOW GOD'S PLAN CAN CHANGE OUR LIVES

Encouraging Word: *God wants to do incredible things in your life.*
Everyday Step: *Decide to seek God's guidance today.*

Do not conform any longer to the pattern of this world, but be transformed by the renewing of your mind. Then you will be able to test and approve what God's will is— his good, pleasing and perfect will.
—*Romans 12:2*

*S*everal months ago I received a key in the mail. It was in a small advertising envelope labeled "key to luxury." For a fleeting moment my heart leaped into my throat, and I thought I had won something. I had the *key*! Silly as it sounds now, for just a second or two I thought the key was special. Life is often like that. Many of us would welcome the appearance of a magical key to unlock instructions for our lives. We want to live fully, doing what we were created to do.

Amazingly, each of us *does* have the key to unlock the life God has planned for us. We have the key to living a full and meaningful and enjoyable life—even if we do not yet realize it. The answers are right before us. They may not always seem easy, but they are beautifully simple. They point to a plan for our lives well beyond what we can imagine.

This is a fine sentiment, but it tends to get trampled by daily life. We try to do the right thing and to live with hope. But roadblocks and detours lead us astray. We often refuse to believe God has great things in store for us. We lean toward worry and negative thoughts. In our confusing, complicated world, opinions, ideas, and beliefs are extremely varied. Get a half dozen people together, and you can come up with three dozen opinions on any given subject. But all of us seem to agree that we end up in the slowest grocery line and that we never find a good parking place. Oddly, even people with great lives and immense blessings expect to make the wrong choice or believe things won't continue to go right.

How in the World Did This Way of Thinking Develop?

The Bible contains a wonderful promise that is the key for our everyday lives: God has a perfect plan for each of us. A *good, pleasing, and perfect* plan. That sounds like something that will go terribly *right*. Many of us are hungry to live out this divine plan—the one customized just for us—but a great promise can turn into a source of concern and even fear. What if we get it wrong? What if we miss it altogether? Why are we so restless?

For life to blossom into what it can be, we must quit conforming to what the world pushes us to do. We need to allow ourselves the pleasure of being transformed by God—even if that pleasure is sometimes mixed with pain. We must learn to tune in to what God is telling us, to understand the nudge of God in our daily lives—and to know if something goes wrong, God can make it right.

Learning to Know and Do God's Will Takes Time

Knowing God's will does not usually come with a burning bush or handwriting on the wall. Instead, it is like any other ability we want to develop: We must pray, focus on it, learn specific skills, and practice. This all happens by moving forward one step at a time. Restlessness is not God's will for our lives—and Murphy really is not to blame. We must change the way we think. We must open our hearts to a better way. While I do not always know what God wants me to do on any given day, I am pretty sure that pulling the covers over my head and groaning is not the starting point for greatness, nor is believing that whatever *can* go wrong *will* go wrong. What kind of life is that?

And yet, many of us feel uncomfortable discussing God's will. We feel a bit like children playing dress-up—as though knowing and doing God's will is something for super-spiritual people who wind up as missionaries. Sometimes it seems easier just to take care of the day's business, then head home to assemble a meal and fall onto the couch. It can be downright hard to know what God wants us to do—because we are the people we are. We are busy. We are stubborn. We find it difficult to trust God with our daily lives. We want to be in control. We are selfish. And that's just the short list.

But side-by-side with these traits is a deep desire to do something great with our lives, to hope, and to enjoy.

At Our Core, We Need to Seek God's Will

This goes far beyond a self-centered desire or a wish list. It is a need that haunts us, a question we were created to answer. We search for the best next step. Following God's will as it unfolds makes life rich and full and shapes us to have impact on the world around us.

While we are hobbling along, we can return again and again to this good news: God has a plan for each of us, and it is not some mysterious recipe to be prepared only by those with holy status. This plan is pleasing, and it works out for our good. Take a look again at Romans 12:2, mentioned at the beginning of this chapter: "Do not conform any longer to the pattern of this world, but be transformed by the renewing of your mind. Then you will be able to test and approve what God's will is—his good, pleasing and perfect will." As we walk through life, we need a sense of direction. This Scripture provides that and helps keep us on track. The words are a reminder again and again that there *is* a good, pleasing, and perfect will for each of us. Keep repeating those words until they are seared on your heart and help shape your daily life. Knowing this is God's plan makes our journey less frightening, more certain.

Or, consider this beautiful passage from the Old Testament book of Jeremiah: "This is what the LORD says: 'Stand at the crossroads and look; ask for the ancient paths, ask where the good way is, and walk in it, and you will find rest for your souls'" (6:16). These words are akin to a modern-day global positioning system—get your bearings, ask for the good way, and walk in it. The words come with a guarantee most mapping programs do not have: follow this path, and you will find rest for your soul.

People I encounter at workshops want this most of all— rest for the soul. We know at some level that such rest comes in doing what God wants us to do. We want to live abundantly, feel happiness, do what we are called to do, love others, and leave the world a bit better because we passed through. This verse is a good road map to help meet those desires day-to-day. Add Romans 12:2, and you have a potent prescription for changing your life.

Take a Fresh Look

Consider where you are in your life and what brings you joy. Be open to serving others and see who appears on your path. Think about what is not working in your life and needs immediate correction. If we acknowledge that God has a plan for our lives, how do we find it? If we feel our great need, how do we satisfy it? Life is complicated, and it takes us in many directions. Even with our best efforts, this feels at times like a cosmic wrestling match. Life has us pinned to the floor.

To start, take a fresh look at your life. Step back and assess how you spend your time and energy each day. Perhaps you need to reconsider your job, for example, and how you are shaping your workday. You may have forgotten what drew you to your career in the first place. Or maybe you will see that you need to spend more time on key family relationships. See what seems to be going right and what needs work. How might God be speaking through your current situation?

As you begin to ponder, pray. Perhaps you believe you cannot pray. Maybe praying seems too hard, even selfish. Sometimes people say they feel as if God is not answering them or they are talking to a brick wall. This is not a deal killer. Your first prayers might be simple: "Guide me, God." "Show me the perfect plan for my life." "Give me insight into how I am to spend my life." Or the old standby: "Help!" Boldly—or tentatively—ask God to show you the perfect will for your life. Ask for your mind to be renewed. You will find "A Prayer for Your Journey" at the end of each chapter in this book to help you get started, and in chapter 4 you will find more details about building a strong prayer life. Begin to plant seeds of prayer, and watch how God nurtures them.

Consider writing prayers and reflecting each day on how God might be answering them. What do you notice happening? When I pray and reflect in my journal, for example, I often see a new direction in which God led me or a personal trend I needed to consider. Or I may identify a nagging problem I need to deal with so I can move on.

Do not be dismayed if you feel distance at times between you and God. Many people experience spiritual dry spells. We are frail and sometimes foolish. We are tempted and often tired. These tough times of searching can help us grow. God wants more for you and will not leave you hanging. "The Lord appeared to us in the past, saying: 'I have loved you with an everlasting love; I have drawn you with loving-kindness'" (Jeremiah 31:3).

Keep trying, putting one foot before the other, moving along with hope. Keep at it. Notice how life unfolds. God wants you to understand the plan for your life and to use this plan to live with more contentment and meaning. If you stop trying, you are like one of those cool classic cars that people keep under a canvas cover in their garage—seldom put to good use.

Turn to the Bible on your journey. You will find the pages of this book filled with Scripture. Be open to how a verse might speak to you at a given point in your life.

Perhaps most important, decide simply that you want to know and do God's will. Give this your best shot—so you can become the person you were meant to be.

The Gospel of John, in chapter 5, tells a fascinating story about an invalid who lies by a healing pool in Jerusalem with many other disabled people each day. On a trip to Jerusalem,

Jesus sees this man and learns that he has been in this condition for nearly four decades. As the scene unfolds, Jesus asks the man an unusual question: "Do you want to get well?" When you read this story, it seems obvious the man wants to get well. However, he does not answer the question. Instead he says he is unable to get into the healing pool; he has no one to carry him; and when he tries to get in, someone else always gets in front of him. The man almost seems to believe it is not possible for him to get well. He is living his own version of Murphy's Law—no one to help, can't get in, not likely to happen.

What Jesus does next shows what can happen in our lives when we are open to the power of God: "Then Jesus said to him, 'Get up! Pick up your mat and walk.' At once the man was cured; he picked up his mat and walked."

In considering this passage and how I live my daily life, I wonder if God is asking the same question of me, and what my answer is.

The Call to Bigger Things

Sione Tu'uta, a United Methodist pastor who grew up in the country of Tonga, says the story in John reminds us that God is calling *each of us* to bigger things. To take advantage of these opportunities, we, like the man by the pool, must prepare for what God has for us in the day ahead and must be in a place where we can encounter Christ. Instead of being afraid of our restlessness, Tu'uta suggests using it as motivation to take inventory and say, "I believe I was created for greater than this."

His position: "Be ridiculous and radical in what God is doing in your life."

I believe I *am* called to do astonishing things, to show what God can do through my everyday life. I want more *for* God, *through* God, *of* God. This means I must depend on God to help me take the best next steps. I must ask for God's help in moving beyond excuses. My excuses sound different from those of the man by the pool ("I am so busy; I have to earn a living; I have so many daily details to take care of; I have other responsibilities"), but their meaning is the same. I wince when I realize how I let excuses get in the way of God's will. But when I acknowledge this shortcoming, I begin to move forward.

Ponder the questions God asks in your life. Are you ready to answer yes? If so, what actions do you want to take this day, this year?

God heals us and empowers us to "get up," to do what we are meant to do. This is what the Creator of the universe wants for us. Christ has "saved us and called us to a holy life—not because of anything we have done but because of his own purpose and grace" (2 Timothy 1:9).

What does a holy life look like in these busy days? Do you believe that God has a purpose for you?

While God's will may seem fuzzy and just out of reach, the opposite is actually true. God lays out basic guidelines for us, just the way we lay out basic rules for our children. We will explore these rules in the coming pages. At the core of them all is the Great Commandment: We must love God with all our heart, soul, and mind, and love others as ourselves. In the context of this commandment, we make hundreds of daily decisions. We try our best, and we are forgiven when we fail.

Once we begin to sense God's will for our lives, we can consider how to live this will. This seems to be where a giant disconnect occurs for many of us—the place between *knowing* and *doing* God's will. That is when Murphy's Law overtakes us. *Doing* God's will can be tough. We are overwhelmed by the details of daily life; a spiritual path eludes us. But this journey can make life so much richer and more enjoyable. It can transform each of us from a person who muddles through to an individual who makes a difference and exudes joy.

Henry David Thoreau wrote, "In the long run, men hit only what they aim at." God's will may seem like a moving target on many days, sometimes for entire seasons of our lives. But I find that when I keep the target in mind, I feel better in my own skin, as though I am truly plugged into the power of God. I know I cannot do everything, so I need to do what I am supposed to do. I find that I accomplish what I focus on. When I focus on *everything*, I accomplish *nothing*. When I focus on *nothing*, I accomplish *nothing*.

Paul, in his Letter to the Philippians, had the right idea: "Whatever you have learned or received or heard from me, or seen in me—put it into practice. And the God of peace will be with you" (Philippians 4:9).

Prepare to change your way of thinking—expect better things to happen, enjoy God's plan for your life, and bid Murphy farewell.

A Prayer for Your Journey

Dear God, thank you for my life. Thank you for this day. A new day—what a gift! You are a generous and loving God, and I thank you and ask you to continue to guide me and help me grow in you. I want to do your good and perfect and pleasing will. Please help me know what and how on a daily basis, on a moment-to-moment basis. In the gracious name of Christ, amen.

Chapter Two

TAKE HOPE

GOD WANTS GOOD THINGS FOR YOUR LIFE

Encouraging Word: *We are created to live with hope
at the core of our being.*
Everyday Step: *Expect good things to happen today.*

*"No eye has seen, no ear has heard, no mind has conceived
what God has prepared for those who love him."*
1 Corinthians 2:9

*W*hen we are young we seem to hope intuitively—we
expect things to go our way. We hope Santa will bring what
we want for Christmas and hope our best friend will get to
spend the night and hope we get ice cream after supper and
hope we get to see a fun movie this weekend.

When I take my young granddaughter to the park, she
fairly explodes from the car, dancing around, going from one
swing set to another, from a yellow slide here to a climbing
wall there, moving from place to place with a certainty that
is nothing if not hopeful. She is optimistic that each of these
toys will be fun and that the other children, even those she
does not know, will want to play with her and that this is
going to be the *best* day.

Her face sparkles with a happiness that reflects this hope.

The years tend to erode such an attitude in us, however.
As the busyness of life and the pressures of decisions and the
memories of times when things did not work out press upon

us, we choose to give up hope. We need to change that. We can infuse our lives with a new spirit.

One of the most powerful words to help us figure out God's will and live joyfully is the word *hope*. This word promises possibilities and options and outcomes that make us happy. The word is so strong and vibrant that it almost seems to need an exclamation point behind it. However, in our day-to-day lives we often train ourselves *not* to hope. If we do hope, we fear we will be disappointed or perhaps look silly.

God has created us to live with hope at the core of our being—with a way of thinking that anticipates rather than dreads. This does not mean walking around like a smiley-face cartoon character; it does mean making decisions and reacting to situations with grace and joy. How can we possibly know and do God's will if we are not hopeful people? How can we move forward in love and certainty if we do not believe things will work out right, good, with meaning?

When we push hope to the side or give up on hope, we are giving up a key tool to moving forward as God wants us to. Having hope does not mean we will never mess up or suffer loss. It does mean God will be with us.

There is an optimism born of hope, giving us energy, enthusiasm, and momentum. This optimism helps us keep going on the days when we really would rather get under our desk and suck our thumbs. It is a forceful motivator in a busy world.

Hope is also a great antidote for worry. When we are hopeful, we find it much more difficult to make room for worry. We expect good things to happen. We are eager to see what unfolds next, instead of dreading it.

This shift in how we look at life can change everything for the better. Suddenly things seem a bit easier. Little things do not bother us so much. Big things seem manageable. On the days when I live with this idea in mind, I am much calmer and happier. I enjoy the day more. Instead of trying to control the world around me and force everything to work my way, I change myself instead. I relax. I am amazed at how this works in my daily life. When I live with hope, things go better. When I expect the worst or complain about how things are unfolding, I am restless, aggravated, fretful.

Some people are afraid to live with this kind of hope, because they think they will look shallow or be called a Pollyanna. This does not have to be the case. Living with a hopeful spirit does not mean we expect only good in our lives. It does not mean we will never experience pain or grief. It means we know good things will be woven into the hurt and loss. We have a power within to help us cope with what life brings. This power is part of God's love and plan for us. In addition, we begin to realize that if something bad does happen, God will make it right. We will know how to deal with it at the time, and we will grow from it. We will be much less fearful.

A little bird showed me how this can work—really, a little bird. It flew inside the screened porch at our cabin on the lake, a cute little nuthatch that somehow had managed to find an opening into the house. Of course, once on the porch it was terrified and could not get out. After watching the bird huddle in a corner, we realized it was not likely to find freedom. My husband, Paul, propped the door open, providing the perfect escape route—still, nothing. Finally Paul corralled it, and the bird flew out. Like the bird, we may find ourselves trapped in a situation we did not anticipate. And instead of looking for the freedom of a new way, we shrink into a corner and expect the worst. We must look beyond what is right in front of us, knowing that God wants to liberate us.

Living with outrageous, radical, enthusiastic hope can be difficult. Life can easily draw us away from it—to worry, to negative habits, to a belief that we live under a cloud and the sun will not come out. But once you start living with hope, you don't want to go back. The world opens up, and the power of God seems more noticeable in daily life.

Here are some ideas for getting started:

Remind yourself many times daily to expect the best and to know that God has good plans for you.

Do not lump life into a hopeless blob. Instead, when something does not go as you had hoped, assess what worked, what didn't, and why. One disappointment does not mean that nothing will ever go right again.

Look at the good in each day, instead of focusing on what went wrong.

Pray and ask for God's reminders of hope. In the Letter to the Romans, we are told that God is the God of hope: "May the God of hope fill you with all joy and peace as you trust in him, so that you may overflow with hope by the power of the Holy Spirit" (Romans 15:13). By trusting in God, we can be filled with joy and peace and *overflow with hope*. This happens by the power of God's spirit in our lives, the presence of one who is so much greater than we are and who is with us no matter what struggles we face. *This* is cause for hope!

Turn to the Psalms, which offer hope and a multitude of good things. These verses can open our hearts and encourage us when we feel low. They can be a great starting point, too, for new readers of the Bible. Words from the Psalms are often tender and personal; they remind us God is with us on this journey and good things are part of the plan. We must learn to draw on this encouragement; for some reason it does not come naturally to us. Here is a sampling of words from the Psalms:

"We wait in hope for the LORD; *he is our help and our shield. In him our hearts rejoice, for we trust in his holy name. May your unfailing love rest upon us, O* LORD, *even as we put our hope in you." (Psalm 33:20-22)*

"Find rest, O my soul, in God alone; my hope comes from him. He alone is my rock and my salvation; he is my fortress, I will not be shaken. My salvation and my honor depend on God; he is my mighty rock, my refuge. Trust in him at all times, O people; pour out your hearts to him, for God is our refuge." (Psalm 62:5-8)

"I lift up my eyes to the hills—where does my help come from? My help comes from the LORD, *the Maker of heaven and earth. He will not let your foot slip—he who watches over you will not slumber. . . . The* LORD *will keep you from all harm—he will watch over your life; the* LORD *will watch over your coming and going both now and forevermore." (Psalm 121:1-3, 7-8)*

Search other Scriptures for reminders that God wants good things for you. Be reassured, for example, by this favorite verse: " 'For I know the plans I have for you,' declares the LORD, 'plans to prosper you and not to harm you, plans to give you hope and a future'" (Jeremiah 29:11). The passage goes on to tell us steps to take: " 'Then you will call upon me and come and pray to me, and I will listen to you. You will seek me and find me when you seek me with all your heart. I will be found by you' " (verses 12-13). Consider this Scripture to be a step-by-step recipe for changing your approach and thinking. Call upon God. Pray. Seek God with all your heart.

I continue to believe God wants better things for us than we can possibly imagine, that the divine plan is for us to enjoy life and live with meaning. We were not created to think small or expect the worst. God has great plans for us.

Ordinary People, Extraordinary Hope

Turning to the New Testament, we find many words of hope from Christ and the people he affected, people just like us. In fact, it's sometimes startling to see the hope these ordinary people showed. Consider those who pressed close to Jesus, just for a glimpse or a touch. Then there were those who crowded around for a word about how to live their lives or to receive healing. They had hope.

Take the woman who had been sick for twelve years with some sort of bleeding disorder. She came up and touched the edge of the cloak of Jesus and was healed. This story contains surprising hope. The woman did not confront Jesus; she came up behind him. She did not try to talk to Jesus:

> She had suffered a great deal under the care of many doctors and had spent all she had, yet instead of getting better she grew worse. When she heard about Jesus, she came up behind him in the crowd and touched his cloak, because she thought, " 'If I just touch his clothes, I will be healed.' " Immediately her bleeding stopped and she felt in her body that she was freed from her suffering." (Mark 5:26-29)

Jesus knew something had happened; he felt her touch despite the many people crowded around him and knew that power had been taken from him. "But Jesus kept looking around to see who had done it. Then the woman, knowing what had happened to her, came and fell at his feet and, trembling with fear, told him the whole truth. He said to her, 'Daughter, your faith has healed you. Go in peace and be freed from your suffering' " (Mark 5:32-34).

This hopeful woman is a minor character in the Bible; we do not even know her name. And yet, she still had enough hope to seek Jesus out and to believe that merely touching his cloak would make the difference. Her hope showed itself as faith, a willingness to take action, to try for healing. And it resulted in her release from suffering. What a great model for our lives!

Sometimes, of course, we lose hope. We become discouraged and afraid. A small voice tells us things will not work out—our business idea is really not unique, or our health is going to hold us back, or we are not smart enough to undertake a new challenge. The list goes on and on. This little voice, though, can be overcome by shifting our perspective to believe good things are going to happen. We can cling to this when we flounder: "Let us hold unswervingly to the hope we profess, for he who promised is faithful" (Hebrews 10:23).

God keeps promises. As our hope grows, our faith grows. We may slip into doubt or fear, but we find that it's easier to come back. We look at the day ahead and believe things are going to be just fine. Or we look at the day just past and know things occurred for a reason and we can build for a new day.

A PRAYER FOR YOUR JOURNEY

Dear Creator, thank you for your promises. I want to be faithful and hopeful as I move through my daily life. Help me adjust my attitude, to trust you and expect good things to happen. Use my life each day to touch others. In the merciful name of Christ, amen.

Chapter Three

GOD'S WORKMANSHIP

STEPS TO BECOMING THE PERSON YOU WERE CREATED TO BE

Encouraging Word: *You are equipped to do something special with your life.*
Everyday Step: *Make a list of things that give you energy.*

*"May the favor of the Lord our God rest upon us;
establish the work of our
hands for us—yes, establish the work of our hands."*
Psalm 90:17

*S*everal years ago I decided to tackle an old fear of mine and ride a horse. The last time I had been on horseback had been about forty years earlier, riding behind my cousin who was gleefully terrorizing me (or so it seemed). Timidly I signed up for a trail ride on a summer vacation, requesting the animal that another guest had deemed too docile. I wanted calm and lots of it. With a little help, I mounted and realized this mare was a lot bigger than she looked from the ground. I immediately felt myself tense up. The group trotted out of the corral, and my horse and I dropped to the back of the line. However, the horse balked and did not want to walk through the gate, past a water hose with a small hissing leak in it. She was not about to get on the path.

The trail master, keeping a close eye on his most timid rider, quickly identified the problem—my nervousness. "She walks past that hose every day," he said, "but she senses your fear. She knows something is wrong; she just can't figure out what it is."

I relaxed, and, sure enough, the horse happily moved along, falling in line as she had done dozens of times before.

Doing what we are uniquely created to do can sometimes seem like this ride. We balk; we are not sure which path to take; we hold back. In doing so, we keep things from unfolding as they should, just as I kept the horse from doing what she knew to do.

We sometimes do not do what we are called to do because we are just not sure. We sense the indifference and stress of the world. We are afraid to go forward, although we cannot pinpoint what is holding us back. We slip and slide. We think we are doing what we are meant to do, but something seems wrong. Sometimes our attitude keeps us from doing what we were designed to do. We may feel as though we are muddling through life.

Created to Do Good Works

We are clearly told that we are the product of God's workmanship, created to do good works. Our lives and very being are touched by the grace of God:

> But because of his great love for us, God, who is rich in mercy, made us alive with Christ even when we were dead in transgressions—it is by grace you have been saved. And God raised us up with Christ and seated us with him in the heavenly realms in Christ Jesus, in order that in the coming ages he might show the incomparable riches of his grace, expressed in his kindness to us in Christ Jesus. For it is by grace you have been saved, through faith—and this not from yourselves, it is the gift of God—not by works, so that no one

can boast. For we are God's workmanship, created in Christ Jesus to do good works, which God prepared in advance for us to do. (Ephesians 2:4-10)

This is thrilling. The power of God resides in each of us, unique and wonderful. God has a job for us to do—and that job is woven into us as surely as our DNA is woven into who we are. We can do something no one else can do.

As you move through life, it may seem as if you are still trying to figure what to be when you grow up. You may be surprised to find yourself struggling to understand what it will take to become the person you were meant to be. Although it sometimes seems to go against what we feel, we are to give up control, turning our days over to God's guidance. In our daily lives, this means relaxing and leaning into what was meant to be, not overthinking it or trying to control every piece of it.

I love a plan more than most people and have been known to go overboard trying to *make* something happen. Galatians 3:3 reproaches me: "Are you so foolish? After beginning with the Spirit, are you now trying to attain your goal by human effort?" In my Bible's margin, I wrote, "me, control freak" and the date as a reminder that I am not to try to make things happen by my own force of will. I have found when I trust God's Spirit, God guides me—even at times when it seems that I am not getting where I think I should be.

One place where we need to let God take over is at work. This means using your time and energy each day in ways you find meaningful and fulfilling. It does not mean, of course, that every day will be fabulous and millions of dollars will pour into your bank account—although miracles do happen. When we trust God to help us find the right work to do, the right way to use the hours we have been given, we often feel contentment and moments of true joy.

What Gives You Energy?

A first step as you consider where God might be leading is to consider what gives you energy—and what *drains* your energy. We are created to do special things—and while these may sometimes be challenging, they are not meant to be a drain.

What charges you up? What makes you feel good, even though you may be tired? What gets you so excited that you want to tell someone about it? What makes you say thank you for the special blessings of a day?

On the flip side, what drains your energy? What frustrates you, despite your best intentions? What wears you out? What makes you feel that you are all thumbs, fumbling in the dark and stubbing your toe along the way?

Take out a sheet of paper and make two lists. What are you spending your time on that matters to you, renews you, or challenges you in a hopeful way? What saps your energy and makes you want to run away and join the circus? Look for patterns and themes.

Here are some of my patterns: I enjoy being with people. I am fired up when given the opportunity to give a speech or lead a retreat. I love to teach my small group at church. I need creative time, time for writing in my journal, and reading. Relationships are very important to me. A family dinner or visits with my granddaughter or young niece always energize me.

From some people, my list would evoke a huge groan. The thought of speaking to three people, much less three hundred, makes them want to throw up. They are happy to organize financial files and make sure the books balance, or to design, set up, and maintain a website. Their list makes me start to twitch, because those items drain my energy.

Aha! We *are* created in different ways. And God is perfectly willing to establish the work of our hands for us, even to help us prosper in our work. In this assessment of what gives us energy, we may begin to get a clearer sense of how God wants us to spend our energy.

What Are You Good At?

In the international terminal at the Atlanta airport, there is an ancient quote from a Latin philosopher. The words are spread out across a very long wall: "Let each man pass his days in that endeavour wherein his gift is greatest." From a distance, the design looks like a huge mosaic. Upon closer examination, we learn that the design is actually made from thousands of colorful business cards. The artwork makes a powerful statement about using our gifts to shape how we use our time.

As a next step in becoming the person you were created to be, consider your strengths and talents. This can be harder than it seems at first glance. Most people quickly say they do not have any talents; they think of playing like a concert pianist or creating an exquisite piece of art. I have never met a person without *many* things he or she is good at. These talents are as varied as the people themselves, and they may be large or small. They may clearly relate to work, or they may be connected to relationships or a hobby.

Sometimes unearthing talents may take effort. The process can be like stripping layers of old paint off a piece of furniture to uncover fine wood beneath. Often through life we pile layer upon layer of chores and responsibilities that cover up what we are really good at—and maybe what we are called to do. At other times, we may find we are right on track but haven't taken time to realize and celebrate that.

Step back and consider what you are good at. Do you have a head for numbers, or do you love words? Is your mind analytical, or do you find yourself coming up with grand "what if" ideas? Are you great at puzzles, planning the details of a vacation, or putting together the family budget? Are you a creative cook who serves meals with both love and flavor? You may be good at getting other people together or at encouraging others. The list could be endless.

The Amazing Power of Spiritual Gifts

A key way to let God establish our work is to discover and use our spiritual gifts. Until a few years ago, I did not understand this. I thought spiritual gifts were for holy people, preachers and Bible scholars, and perhaps an evangelist or two. I did not realize that I had special gifts, given by God and available to help me become the person I was created to be. I took a class at church on identifying personal gifts, and I was astonished. The things I enjoy doing and am good at are directly related to my gifts.

We are not only *called* to do certain things; we are *designed* to do them. As the Bible says: "There are different kinds of gifts, but the same Spirit. There are different kinds of service, but the same Lord. There are different kinds of working, but the same God works all of them in all men" (1 Corinthians 12:4-6).

Lists of spiritual gifts vary slightly, but the basics are outlined in Romans 12:4-8:

> Just as each of us has one body with many members, and these members do not all have the same function, so in Christ we who are many form one body, and each member belongs to all the others. We have different gifts, according to the grace given us. If a man's gift is prophesying, let him use it in proportion to his faith. If it is serving, let him serve; if it is teaching, let him teach; if it is encouraging, let him encourage; if it is contributing to the needs of others, let him give generously; if it is leadership, let him govern diligently; if it is showing mercy, let him do it cheerfully.

This is an easy-to-understand list with God's stamp of approval on it.

Elsewhere in the Bible, the apostle Peter gives a simple synopsis of gifts: "Above all, love each other deeply, because love covers over a multitude of sins. Offer hospitality to one another without grumbling. Each one should use whatever gift he has received to serve others, faithfully administering God's grace in its various forms" (1 Peter 4:8-10). This latter Scripture concisely outlines the importance of using our gifts to serve God. And, like the passage from Romans 12 above, it tells *how* to use each gift—generously, diligently, cheerfully, faithfully, without grumbling, and so on. This is such a loving tutorial from our Lord, nudging us in the right direction, helping us know *and* do.

You may read these lists and pray about them and have an immediate sense of where your strengths are. Or you may consider taking a class at your church or reading a book on spiritual gifts. Perhaps you will want to go online and take a free, Scripture-based assessment to help identify your gifts. For example, the United Methodist Church provides a useful assessment at its website. It is not a test, and there are no right or wrong answers.

Explore more. The Internet offers many similar assessments. A note of caution here: Make certain you use an assessment with a Christian approach, based on biblical truths. These assessments are intended as a starting point on your journey to understand more fully how you were created.

The Reverend David Ewart, minister at Capilano United Church of Canada, has strong thoughts on spiritual gifts and how powerful they can be: "Go where your gifts are; there you will find God. Apart from many useful and practical reasons for discerning your gifts, the most profound reason is simply that your gifts are the place where God is closest to you in your life. Go where your gifts are and you will be closer to the source of those gifts—God." He goes on to say: "Gifts are about living, and living takes a lifetime. Reflecting on one's gifts ought to be a touchstone that we return to again and again—and always in community and conversation."

Gifts cover the complete range of people and talents. I love the idea, for instance, that encouraging is a special gift. You do not need education or a glib tongue or a quick brain to encourage. You merely need to treat others with kindness and mercy and offer them hope in tough times.

Consider again what you enjoy doing and how you enrich the lives of others through your daily actions.

Meeting the Needs of the World

One of the thrilling facts about our gifts is that, besides giving us energy, they help meet a need in the world. Theologian Frederick Buechner, a great source of insight, says our gifts and the world's needs are woven together: "The place where God calls you is the place where your deep gladness and the world's deep hunger meet." The first time I read this quote I nearly jumped out of my chair. God is calling us to a place that not only meets a need but also brings us deep gladness. When these two components meet, watch out.

When I see people using their gifts to help others, I am inspired—people like the man in my hometown who wants to bring peace and God's love to communities one block at a time and uses his gift of leadership to make it happen, or the psychologist I met recently who wants to help everyone redefine what retirement means and make it into a rich spiritual journey, or the volunteers at my church who use their time to offer a free medical clinic.

Sometimes these activities take place in our jobs—what we are paid to do. At other times they are a calling outside of our careers. These callings may change over time, too, as we mature or grow or learn or explore. Our calling is a journey of discovery, not a planned development.

In exploring and living our gifts, we can do mundane, everyday chores with joy when we know we are doing what God wants us to do. I suspect the people I mentioned above have days when things do not seem to be going just right—but they do not give up. And I know there are days when they have things they would rather not do, but they do them anyway. Part of living our gifts is to be obedient—a word we tend to shy away from in modern life. We do not want to obey; we want to do what we want to do when we want to do it. But obey we must if we are to live out God's great plans for our lives.

To summarize:

- Explore your gifts and talents and understand what makes you unique.
- Realize that everyone has gifts. This includes *you*!

• Step back to assess what your strengths are and how they enrich the world.

For some reason, we tend to underestimate God when it comes to our daily lives, even though we are told again and again that *nothing* is beyond God's power. God will guide us. Remember Jeremiah 32:26-27: "Then the word of the LORD came to Jeremiah: 'I am the LORD, the God of all mankind. Is anything too hard for me?' "

Equipped by God

We can trust that God will equip us to do what we are called to do. God equips us through our gifts, but also through God's holy power and might. A wonderful example is in the story of God leading the people of Israel out of Egypt. On the surface this seemed impossible, and the people were afraid.

Take a look at this story in Exodus 14:13-14: "Moses answered the people, 'Do not be afraid. Stand firm and you will see the deliverance the LORD will bring you today. The Egyptians you see today you will never see again. The LORD will fight for you; you need only to be still.'"

Have I mentioned that we need to relax and trust, and things will work out?

Do not hesitate to call upon God to help you with your work situation. The Psalmist wrote in Psalm 90:17: "May the favor of the Lord our God rest upon us; establish the work of our hands for us—yes, establish the work of our hands." In my own career, I find when I pray and diligently seek God's guidance in my work life, I make good decisions. I have a sense of being right where I am supposed to be. God always provides. When I begin to feel I am not in the right spot, I know I must pray for God to establish the work of my hands. The power that comes with this prayer is awesome.

As we move through life, whether we are meandering on a trail or being led across our own Red Sea, we can relax and rely on the knowledge that God made us. Then we can commit ourselves again each day to God—to say we believe, even when things are not perfectly clear, and to make ourselves available to be used by God in any way God chooses. We want to develop and use our gifts to further God's work in this world, whether it be leading a business or encouraging a neighbor or serving someone we encounter in our daily routine.

We are gifted and guided, and that is more than enough. So we decide to say yes to God's will for our lives and the work the Lord wants to do through us. As we work, we struggle and learn, knowing all the while that we are in need of love, wisdom, strength, faith, and forgiveness.

A PRAYER FOR YOUR JOURNEY

Dear Lord, thank you for the unique gifts you have given me and for the uses you have for those gifts. Please help me learn more about my spiritual gifts and find the right places to serve you with those gifts. In the loving name of Christ, amen.

Chapter Four

TALKING WITH GOD, LISTENING TO GOD

HOW PRAYER CAN HELP

Encouraging Word: *God will answer your prayers in exciting and interesting ways.*
Everyday Step: *Set aside time to pray.*

"This is the confidence we have in approaching God: that if we ask anything according to his will, he hears us. And if we know that he hears us—whatever we ask—we know that we have what we asked of him." 1 John 5:14

*S*o often we seem to approach God as though we are on a job interview, sitting across a desk in uncomfortable clothes asking for something we suspect we are not qualified for. We are fairly certain we are not going to get what we ask for and that God is going to say, "I'll get back to you." Seeking to know and do God's will, we find we need to learn how to draw closer to God and relax in this divine presence—and that means communicating with God through prayer.

Many of us grew up praying in very traditional ways, reciting the Lord's Prayer in church or perhaps bowing for a blessing over a meal. Some of us grew up rarely praying at all, feeling that God was far away and inaccessible. Now, as adults, when we realize we badly need the guidance of a loving God, we might find it hard to pray. Our words can sound selfish and shallow, needy and greedy. We wonder how God could care about our home or job when compared with issues such as world peace and cures for major illnesses.

Building a consistent and open prayer life can take us beyond where we dreamed we could go.

God wants our prayers and invites us to ask for guidance and for what we need. Building a prayer life that accompanies the challenges of daily life is a key step in learning how to know and do God's will. Consider James 5:13-14, 16: "Is any one of you in trouble? He should pray. Is anyone happy? Let him sing songs of praise. Is any one of you sick? He should call the elders of the church to pray over him and anoint him with oil in the name of the Lord. . . . The prayer of a righteous man is powerful and effective." *Powerful. Effective.* These words make me want to pray, and they give me hope as I pray.

God has shown me so much through prayer and guided me in exciting and sometimes scary ways. When I pause to think about it, all the answers have helped me live God's will and be the person I was created to be. My need for prayer is immense, and God's willingness to listen and to answer is even bigger. Having kept a journal for decades, I look back and see time after time when God stepped in for me. Some of God's messages have been dramatic and even a bit odd. One time as I started my business, I thought God told me, "You ain't seen nothing yet" and went on to remind me that I am to tell others of God's power. Other messages have been much more subtle. These messages are hard to explain and may not make sense until you begin to pray and to wait for God's nudge.

How Do I Build a Prayer Life?

Building a prayer life sounds so lofty, as though it could take weeks at a retreat center or a degree from seminary. Initiating contact can be a bit overwhelming—not only for those who have never prayed but for those who have prayed and been disappointed or unsure.

Do not be scared off by the thought of a close relationship with God, as if some divine principal will be looking over your shoulder all the time, waiting to call you into the office.

Consider God's great love for you, a divine desire to be close and help with your daily life. As explained in Numbers 23:19: "God is not a man, that he should lie, nor a son of man, that he should change his mind. Does he speak and then not act? Does he promise and not fulfill?"

Begin to consider the kind of relationship you would like to have with the Creator, who loves and forgives and wants great things for you. A relationship with God is not something you order out of a catalog. It will be different for each of us but will likely have similar characteristics. How do you want this relationship with God to look in your daily life? Are you seeking guidance? reassurance? forgiveness? mercy? a deeper understanding of God's spirit? Take time to jot down these thoughts.

Slow down to contemplate this. Of all the things worth our time, prayer goes at the top of our list. Plunge right in with a request for God's spirit to come anew into you, to guide you. This can be scary because obviously we cannot see the spirit of God, and it is hard to understand how it works. But it does. The Bible promises this, and this spirit will guide and comfort you in ways you cannot imagine as you learn to call upon it. In Zephaniah 3:17, these comforting words tell about God's willingness to have a close relationship: "The LORD your God is with you, he is mighty to save. He will take great delight in you, he will quiet you with his love, he will rejoice over you with singing."

To move this relationship along, look at your daily life and the people to whom you are closest. How have those relationships been built? By spending time together, by listening to each other, by enjoying the same things, by valuing what the other person has to offer, by trusting. You depend on these people for support. In turn, you are willing to do what they want and need you to do. You confide in them and ask for their advice. They encourage you.

This is probably the same way you will shape a connection with God. While you may not sit down and hear God's voice over a shared cappuccino, you can learn in peaceful ways to pick up on what God is saying. You are refreshed, calling upon this source of energy.

Realistically, many of us pray when we are desperate. We are afraid we have an illness. We are about to lose someone we love. We have made bad choices that have had terrible results. These are intense, emotional prayers that take courage and shine a tiny ray of God's light somewhere deep within us. People have been praying out of desperation for centuries. Consider such a prayer in Psalm 142:1-3. (This is a good prayer to start with if you are overwhelmed and cannot find words.) "I cry aloud to the LORD; I lift up my voice to the LORD for mercy. I pour out my complaint before him; before him I tell my trouble. When my spirit grows faint within me, it is you who know my way." If you start your prayer like this, there is no turning back. You will find that you turn to God more and more, and you will sense the Lord's guidance in remarkable ways.

Certainly we want to respect and love and revere God. However, God has invited us into a relationship that goes beyond formality, offering us Jesus as our Savior who shows God's love to us. In Proverbs 18:24, we are told there is a friend who is closer than a brother. I am quite close to my brothers; they have walked with me through good and bad, and we have had lots of fun together. Perhaps you think of someone else you are close to—your dearest friend, your mother, your spouse or child. Remember that God wants an intimate relationship with us that is even closer. Prayer is a good way to build that closeness.

Say Thank You

One way to build a relationship with God is to say thank you. Have you ever been surprised by generous thanks from someone, perhaps in the form of an unexpected gift or thoughtful handwritten note? In the same way that we like to be appreciated, God wants us to offer our gratitude for the many blessings in our lives.

Saying thank you to God serves multiple purposes. It helps me remember God is in charge, that everything I have or am I owe to God. It also helps me realize how many blessings I have in my life, even on the bad days. This is a good way to get past Murphy's Law. As we offer our thanks to God, we often begin to have good, positive feelings about what is happening in our lives, rather than focusing on the worst. This, in turn, gives us strength and hope for the next steps in our lives.

This does not mean, of course, that we should go to God wearing rose-colored glasses, giving surface thanks and not expecting God's help on serious and deep issues. To the contrary. If we start with praise and thankfulness, we are better prepared to go deeper in our conversations with God.

How to Pray

How you pray is personal and varied, but it is helpful to refer to *the* model for prayer—the Lord's Prayer. Study it and see what Christ thought was important when he offered it. The prayer acknowledges God as holy and majestic, and Jesus immediately asks for God's will to be done. This business of God's will is important in our lives! He asks that God give us our daily food, a nice reminder Christ cares about our physical needs. He shows our need to ask for forgiveness and to forgive others. (This passage has taken me years to work on; I thought if God was holding the same kinds of grudges and selfish thoughts about me that I was about others, there might be trouble.) Jesus' request that we not be led into temptation but be delivered from evil reminds me regularly how easy it is to slip into negative thoughts, wrong actions, or unkind words. Jesus ends his prayer with another round of praise for God—with strong words of power and glory, forever and ever.

A friend once told me she did not enjoy saying the Lord's Prayer. She said it had become rote, and that the people saying it did not seem to be thinking of its meaning at all. It is easy at times to lapse into praying by formula, not truly thinking about the words—"Bless this food." "Keep us safe." "Watch over the kids." Perhaps this is not all bad, because it helps build a habit of prayer; however, it's good to stop and consider the words we are saying and how they must fall on the ears of God. A few years later, in a discussion about prayer in a small group, another friend mentioned how *much* she loves to pray the Lord's Prayer in church, getting chills to think of God hearing the prayers of all those gathered people. We are different people with different approaches to prayer. God listens. God answers.

Christ teaches many lessons in an intriguing yet straight-forward way, including his down-to-earth ways of explaining prayer. In Matthew 6, for example, Jesus teaches about worry and prayer. I love this lesson because Christ is so certain we don't need to worry about what we will eat or drink or about what we will wear. He tells us in his forthright way that none of us can add a single hour to our lives by worrying. He goes on to say God knows our needs: "For the pagans run after all these things, and your heavenly Father knows that you need them" (Matthew 6:32). The simple language in this verse reminds me that God is in touch with my ordinary life.

As always, though, God's lesson goes farther. It tells me what I must do, and I believe this involves much prayer: "But seek first his kingdom and his righteousness, and all these things will be given to you as well. Therefore do not worry about tomorrow, for tomorrow will worry about itself. Each day has enough trouble of its own" (Matthew 6:33-34). Surely this scripture is one of the best examples of "whatever can go wrong, God can make right."

In Conversation with God

I'm always interested in the students who come to our door, selling a candy bar to raise money for the band at school or cookies for their club. They hesitantly approach the front door, knock nervously, and tell what they are trying to do. Their efforts on behalf of something beyond themselves touches me, and I am happy to help them. This is a reminder of how we can ask God for help. If we have trouble doing so, then we, like the children who have mom or dad along to help, can ask a friend to pray for us. God wants to hear from us, to be in conversation with us about our lives. In Luke 11:9-10, Jesus says: "Ask and it will be given to you; seek and you will find; knock and the door will be opened to you. For everyone who asks receives; he who seeks finds; and to him who knocks, the door will be opened."

When you pray regularly, you feel more comfortable. To start, you might set aside time for prayer in the morning and evening. You might write down prayers and begin to read the Bible as part of prayer time. From there, you can weave prayer into your daily life—wherever you are and whatever you do. This is hands-free conversation, so you can do it as you drive or while at work. As you remember to pray throughout the day, strength comes—a reassurance that you do not have to make everything happen, a peace in knowing that someone else is in control. You may find yourself asking for help with a business decision or praying for one of your children during their school day or saying thanks for a particularly beautiful sunset as you drive home. Somehow, through consistent daily prayer, you will begin to be aware of God in a richer way. You will find yourself nudged and guided through the day, sometimes despite your doubts and fears.

As your prayer life develops, put your trust in God. Sometimes in prayer we ask with hope but then begin to believe it just won't work out. Here comes our friend Murphy again, claiming that our requests are too outlandish or selfish or God has bigger fish to fry. When this happens, consider these verses from Proverbs 3:5-6: "Trust in the LORD with all your heart and lean not on your own understanding; in all your ways acknowledge him, and he will make your paths straight."

God has a better plan for our lives, and we can live it by prayerfully trusting, acknowledging God's presence and watching God straighten out our path. In our daily lives, this may not be easy at first; it takes ongoing practice. It looks a little like what my toddling great-niece did when learning to walk. She would go a few steps, fall down, sometimes cry, sometimes giggle, and then pick herself up and toddle some more. Over the months she became steadier on her feet and knew much more clearly what she was supposed to do. We can do that same thing in learning to pray and seeing the path unfold before us.

However, sometimes we struggle to pray. Have you ever called someone near the end of his or her favorite television show? With static in the background, the person is distracted and annoyed at the interruption and cannot get off the phone fast enough. Approaching God in prayer can sometimes feel like that. We may feel as though we are bothering God, or we ourselves may be confused and have trouble sorting out our thoughts. Give your confusion to God, in whatever way you can. Say, "Help!" Write your concerns on a piece of paper or in your journal and lay them symbolically before God. Ask a friend to pray for you. If you are in a small group or class at church, ask for the group to pray for you, giving as many or as few details as you feel comfortable doing.

Tapping into God's Spirit

If we want to build a strong prayer life, God offers comforting yet puzzling help in the Holy Spirit. I use the word puzzling because I find it tough at times to grasp the immensity of God's presence and communicate with it. The Bible tells us that the Holy Spirit can offer prayers for us when we do not know where to start: "The Spirit helps us in our weakness. We do not know what we ought to pray for, but the Spirit himself intercedes for us with groans that words cannot express. And he who searches our hearts knows the mind of the Spirit, because the Spirit intercedes for the saints in accordance with God's will" (Romans 8:26-27). This promise stretches my mind, but it also is a reminder that the power of God goes beyond what I can imagine.

Another way to build a strong prayer life is to get into the habit of praying for other people. Listen when people voice their needs. Say a prayer for them. Jot down a list of prayer concerns others have expressed to you, and pray for those. Many churches have a prayer room where people gather regularly to pray, and you may want to get involved there.

Recently I met a wonderful, godly woman who said she keeps a prayer basket filled with the written requests for prayer that she has heard. She prints out e-mails and jots down notes, then puts these in a basket and prays for all the requests each day. She then pulls out one request and offers a special prayer for that person all day; she also looks for ways to minister to that person all day. Such a practice can help us develop our own gifts and become more loving and focused on other people. We offer a gift when we pray for people. When we give something away, we grow in the process.

Pray each day, steadily, regularly, for things big and little. Remember that God is listening and wants good things for you. Whatever happens, the spirit of God is there, ready to be tapped into.

A Prayer for Your Journey

Dear God, thank you for hearing my prayers. Please help me learn to listen for your answers. Guide my thoughts and words and actions as I try to do what you want me to do. In the name of Christ, who listens, amen.

Chapter Five

IMPATIENT FOR CHANGE

HOW TO WAIT FOR GOD'S GUIDANCE

Encouraging Word: *Waiting can be a time of rest and renewal.*
Everyday Step: *Postpone a decision you are not ready to make.*

"I waited patiently for the LORD; he turned to me and heard my cry." Psalm 40:1

When I try to open a file on my computer, I expect it to appear immediately. When it does not, I hit the enter button again—and again. The result is that my computer slows down even more, and the files take longer to open. I wind up spending time closing what I did not need. I become frustrated. This is an annoying habit that I should break.

Sometimes I sense this same approach in turning to God for guidance. I find myself and many of the people I encounter impatient for answers. We keep hitting the enter key without giving God enough time to work.

We acquire this unhelpful approach in our daily lives. We like instant information and a quick response to every request. Dial-up Internet access becomes too slow, so we move to DSL. Then we get a chance for *faster* DSL, and Murphy's Law rears its ugly head. We are too rushed to go into the bank or pharmacy, so we go to the drive-through.

We have multiple lanes to choose from. The one we choose seems to move too slowly, so we crane our neck, assess which one is moving faster, and strategize a swift lane change. Then a car pulls in behind us and we sigh, frustrated that our new plan did not work. It is no wonder that we want God's immediate response to our needs and desires.

Learning to Wait

One of the hardest parts of seeking God's perfect plan for our lives is learning to wait. Once we start seeking the plan, we want it instantly. Heaven forbid that we might have to wait for it to be revealed and then wait for it to unfold.

Learning to wait can be fulfilling, helping prepare us for whatever God has in store. Waiting can help us grow in ways that we might never have expected, and it can enhance the prayer life we discussed in chapter 4. Before we talk about the sweetness of waiting, however, we need to brush up on what it takes to learn the skill of waiting. I have never found this easy, but I have found it to be worth the effort.

Learning to wait comes through prayer and Bible study, but it also comes through learning to trust God each day. While I usually want things to happen *now*, I am learning to trust God that events will happen in God's time. This may seem trite, until you look back at your life and see the many ways in which the hand of God was at work. For example, I consider jobs I did not take, moves I did not make, frenzies that I allowed to fizzle, issues that did not need my time or me. In some cases I put off decisions I did not need to make yet, either because I did not have enough information to make them wisely, because I had a niggling sense of doubt, or because I had not done the necessary preparation.

Preparation for following God's guidance is a step that people tend to overlook. They get ready for the big decision—the jump off the high-diving board—but have not considered what they need to do before jumping. Don't take the plunge if you haven't learned to swim, checked to make sure the pool is deep enough, or put on your swimsuit! Similarly, if you're considering a job change, don't make the big leap before assessing your income, checking to see if your spouse or significant other is supportive, and making sure you have the skills for a new role. Preparation has been a challenge in my own life, where my impatience has sometimes propelled me to change more quickly than would have been prudent.

Move steadily along, instead of acting like a daredevil trying to jump over a canyon. The Bible is full of "wait" messages, and they pop out regularly when I am trying to make a decision or listen to God. Over the years, I've learned that the way for me to follow God is to slow down, stop trying to get ahead of God, and let things unfold naturally. This is the antithesis of the Murphy's Law approach, which shoves us along, making us believe we had better do something *now* or all our chances will be lost. Listen to the psalmist: "I wait for you, O LORD; you will answer, O Lord my God" (Psalm 38:15).

While waiting, we can live our daily lives in ways that prepare us for what is ahead—including all the breathtaking things God has in store for us. Perhaps we are building our faith, watching surprising strength and courage emerge: "Wait for the LORD; be strong and take heart and wait for the LORD" (Psalm 27:14). Perhaps we are growing to have greater influence on others for God. I think here of 1 Timothy 4:15: "Be diligent in these matters; give yourself wholly to them so that everyone may see your progress. Watch your life and doctrine closely. Persevere in them, because if you do, you will save both yourself and your hearers."

Consider stories of those in the Bible who waited: David, who had secretly been named king and yet served Saul, putting his own plans on hold; Jacob, who worked for seven years to earn the hand of the woman he loved; Esther, who became queen and was willing to risk her life to save her people.

Besides having a perfect plan for us, God knows our weaknesses, including the knowledge that we can be pushy and stamp our feet when we do not immediately get what we want. A verse that has recently spoken to my impatience is Psalm 69:5: "You know my folly, O God; my guilt is not hidden from you." When I realize a bit sheepishly that the Good Shepherd knows how goofy I can be, I am able to turn to God for help not only with my actions but also with my attitude.

My husband and I took an anniversary trip to South America, and sometimes we found ourselves unsure of what to do because we do not speak Spanish. We were thankful for outstanding local guides who greeted us at airports and helped us get where we needed to go. We stepped into busy concourses, looking for a sign with our name on it, expecting someone would be there to help us. Had we rushed out and tried to find our own way, confusion would have reigned.

It reminded me of my relationship with God. As I contemplate how hard it is for me to wait in my life, I realize that God is my great guide, who knows my weaknesses and shows up for me wherever I am. I do not have to doubt this. He translates for me and steers me to the right place at the right time. Because of God's guidance, waiting does not have to be a time of dread but can be a time of hope.

Why Wait?

Waiting for God can actually renew rather than drain. Notice the words of Isaiah: "Do you not know? Have you not heard? The LORD is the everlasting God, the Creator of the ends of the earth. He will not grow tired or weary, and his understanding no one can fathom. He gives strength to the weary and increases the power of the weak. Even youths grow tired and weary, and young men stumble and fall; but those who hope in the LORD will renew their strength. They will soar on wings like eagles; they will run and not grow weary, they will walk and not be faint" (Isaiah 40:28-31).

The last verse of this passage is often quoted, but consider each of the verses, woven together to remind us that God understands us more than we can comprehend. In some versions, verse 31 says those who *wait* for the Lord are renewed. Waiting and hope are sometimes interchangeable, a fantastic reminder for our daily lives. In discussing this passage with a young pastor, I learned that when the verses speak of soaring, they mean wings opened wide, a majestic show. And the reference to running means running *all out*— the kind you did when you were a kid. This is some kind of renewal!

If we hope as we wait, all will be well: "No one whose hope is in you will ever be put to shame" (Psalm 25:3). Instead of looking at waiting as a tedious trial, look at it as a time to be renewed, to collect your thoughts, to consider great blessings ahead. Words about waiting abound in the Scriptures, and you can apply them to your current situation.

Waiting can keep us from rushing into the wrong decision. Remember the wise words from Ecclesiastes 3:1, 11: "There is a time for everything, and a season for every activity....

He has made everything beautiful in its time." Sometimes we get so frustrated with our daily lives that we want to do something, *anything,* to move forward. Consider instead turning to Scripture and praying for God's guidance in how to deal with your impatience.

Waiting can help slow the frenzy of the world and give you a fresh perspective when you are uncertain. Consider two scriptures: "I wait for the LORD, my soul waits, and in his word I put my hope" (Psalm 130: 5). "The Lord is not slow in keeping his promise, as some understand slowness" (2 Peter 3:9). These verses remind us to believe in Christ and that at times we simply may not understand God's timing. Oswald Chambers, in *My Utmost for His Highest* (which I highly recommend), writes: "When God brings the blank space, see that you do not fill it in but wait.... Wait for God to move."

Waiting can help keep us from proceeding when we are in doubt. Sometimes waiting may cause us to turn around. The prophet Elijah wanted to hear from God, and God spoke quietly, saying in part: " 'Go back the way you came.' " And then God gave Elijah specific instructions. Retracing our footsteps may be part of waiting, considering what has worked and what has not.

Praying for Patience

Still having a tough time waiting? Then pray for patience. I have sometimes been amused to hear faithful believers tell people *not* to pray for patience, because they might get it! *Not* praying for patience is giving in to the Murphy's Law mindset. In fact, it might be called a believer's corollary to Murphy's Law, and we need to move beyond it. If you are struggling, ask God for patience. Perhaps something astonishing will grow out of this effort. Remember in James where we are told that waiting can help make us mature and complete. And in Romans 8:25: "But if we hope for what we do not yet have, we wait for it patiently."

Praying for patience might help you build strength because in waiting you learn not to waver. People who have the gift of waiting with patience and grace seem to radiate this steadfast spirit, one that comes with peacefulness. The Reverend Ellen Alston, an associate pastor at the church I attend, comes to mind. Ellen's home and church were destroyed by Hurricane Katrina, and she had to relocate, rebuild, and reconnect. Her patient approach inspires me still. I also think of my friend Rita, who exudes joyful patience in her daily life, as though she is watching a flower slowly blossom, knowing the result is worth the wait.

Take another look at a Psalm that is familiar, this time considering it a prayer for help as you wait: "Create in me a pure heart, O God, and renew a steadfast spirit within me. Do not cast me from your presence or take your Holy Spirit from me. Restore to me the joy of your salvation and grant me a willing spirit, to sustain me" (Psalm 51:10-12).

If you really really really find yourself having trouble waiting, don't be afraid to ask God if this might be a time to act quickly. Even though God may have something else in store for you, the Bible clearly tells us we are to ask for what we need. I am drawn to the psalmist, for example, who says, "Answer me, O LORD, out of the goodness of your love; in your great mercy turn to me. Do not hide your face from your servant; answer me quickly, for I am in trouble" (Psalm 69:16-17). I take heart in being able to turn to God for an answer, calling on great mercy and putting into words my troubles.

When God guides you, you will know it. Then it is time to get to work, to move on, to tackle a task, or to make a decision. Do not drag your heels once you are sure. Instead, trust God, who says to us in Isaiah 46:11: "What I have said, that will I bring about; what I have planned, that will I do."

A Prayer for Your Journey

Dear Heavenly God, please help me as I wait for your guidance. Lead me to make the right decisions at the right time. Forgive my impatience. In the miraculous name of Christ, amen.

Chapter Six

DO LESS, BE MORE

OPENING UP SPACE FOR GOD'S HELP

Encouraging Word: *You are not called to do everything
for everyone.*
Everyday Step: *Say no to something that is going to
overload your schedule.*

"I have stilled and quieted my soul." Psalm 131:2

I signed up for a week of classes at a retreat center in the
Midwest awhile back. When I made the travel arrangements,
I discovered that to get an affordable plane ticket, I needed
to stay over the weekend after the classes ended. I made the
reservations, thinking how nice it would be to have a little
R&R time after a week of workshops, time when I could
read and pray and enjoy some solitude.

However, as the trip grew closer, I got more and more
antsy. I called the airline several times to see if I could
arrange an earlier return without an expensive fee. When I
arrived at the lovely retreat center, I thought for a moment
or two how glad I was to have the extra days—and then
began to try to figure out how to leave sooner.

Throughout my life—and the lives of many of those I
encounter—I see this kind of attitude, like a child who finds
it hard to sit still. I keep going and doing. I often find it hard
to relax and enjoy the rich, unexpected moments life yields.

That, of course, is just the kind of time I had at the end of
the week at the retreat center—rich and unexpected. My

classmates left for various parts of the country, and I wished again for an earlier flight. Then slowly I began to change my attitude about staying, deciding to savor the time apart and alone. I wandered through the grounds, appreciating the beautiful sunshine, the waving grasses, and the variety of birds that were singing. I discovered a small gazebo with a porch swing and climbing red roses and sat there with my journal and Bible, amazed at God's goodness. Toward the end of the day I crossed paths with an elderly woman in a wheelchair, who smiled at the beauty of the evening and said, "Aren't we fortunate?"

In my life, there have been many times such as this when I have sensed God reminding me *to do less and be more.* In all our lives, if we are to do God's will and live fully, we must learn to clear out room for God. If every moment is full of noise and activity, God's voice is hard to hear—and our God is a God who rarely just barges in.

Making choices that honor our priorities and our intention to know and do God's will is a spiritual discipline.

Through my own life and working with others, I have realized it is nearly impossible to do God's will if we are hurrying and worrying too much. I observed this in how I went about each day and wrote a book about my journey. This book led to conversations with individuals all over the country, who confirmed similar findings in their lives. I am passionate about this topic and know that hurry and worry can destroy our joy and our relationship with the Lord. Even so, I will be the first to admit that it takes constant focus to overcome these habits. It is *not* something we do once and never have to think about again.

Discerning God's will is a difficult skill to practice when we are especially busy. In Psalm 119:125, we read: "I am your servant; give me discernment that I may understand

your statutes." We won't reach the psalmist's level of understanding if we are running around in a frenzy all the time.
Imagine that your mind is your favorite room in the house.
Imagine the room as you love it, when it is clean and organized and welcoming. Now, begin to add things to the room—
a chair that wouldn't fit in another room, piles of paperwork
here and there, a rickety table that is piled high with books
and magazines, a basket of unfolded laundry. Before long,
you would not even want to venture into the room. It certainly would not be your favorite. That's the way our
mind looks when we so clutter it that we do not allow
space to follow God.

The Overload of Overscheduling

Time overload often comes incrementally; we think
adding one more little thing to our schedules will not matter.
This is like adding weights to the machine at the gym. Five
pounds does not *seem* like much until you add five more and
five more and five more. Before long you cannot even move.

Most people have so many areas of their lives that require
time and energy. They make family and job and career decisions many times each day, all with the potential to put a
hefty load on their calendars. Then they have their volunteer
activities, helping with church projects and civic groups and
schools.

As we overload our schedules, we also overload our
minds, resulting in what granddaughter Gracie innocently
calls "too many thinkings." We have so many thoughts
racing around in there that we forget things, both big and
little. At home, we set out to get something—and by the
time we arrive in the next room we cannot recall what we

needed. Our mind often tries to draw us back to busyness, back to the details of the day: chores, errands, doing something, planning something. This leaves little space for godly direction.

Frequently my own schedule gets overfull; it looks like a calendar on steroids. As I look through my journals, I find entries such as these: "I am working on my perennial goal: do less" and "I am doing way too much. How to simplify?" When I make these entries, I know I must come before God to quiet my overstimulated soul. A good first step is to say thank you to God—for great love, grace, mercy, and forgiveness, and for listening during busy moments.

Regularly during his ministry, Christ stepped back to allow room for the voice of God. He withdrew from crowds. He prayed. He relied on a few key people to help him do this. Jesus certainly had plenty he *could* have been doing— all those people crowding around, sermons to preach, miracles to perform. But he knew that he needed time away.

When the world crowds in, we need space to absorb God's grace and guidance; this space is a tool to help us know God's will. Time apart can allow us, with God's help, to pull ourselves together.

Saying No

For many people, the reason they're so busy is that they simply cannot say no. Learning to utter this tiny and powerful word seems to be one of the hardest lessons of all. Yet saying no to some things is imperative if we are to say yes to God's will.

Here are some things to keep in mind about saying no:

Understand you are not called to do everything for

everyone. Use your special gifts in ways that show love. Act with tenderness and kindness and patience, not in impatient, rushed ways.

Learn not to blurt out yes when you are already so busy you cannot do anything else. One way to manage this is to say you want to consider the assignment before you commit to it. Pray about it. Sleep on it. See if you feel led to do it or if it is something you feel obligated to do. (We all have times when we take on something to be nice or because we want to help; however, consistently taking on too much can drain us of our effectiveness in areas where we are gifted and most useful.)

When you say yes, you are making a decision to add something else to your calendar—and your busy mind. **Ask yourself if this is something you have time and energy to do.**

If you have trouble saying no, here are some suggestions:

Make a list of reasons that express why choices may not be right for you. Your list can be used to convince both yourself and others. The list might include: "I am committed to other projects, and I could not do justice to this." "I have made a promise to myself to spend more time with my family." "I appreciate invitations to serve, but I am overextended at the moment." "I am trying to put my time and energy into areas that I am best suited for, and I do not feel as though this is one."

Always consider what God would have you do in a situation. Pray about it. Sometimes we say yes with the best of intentions. We want to serve and help and be useful and loving. However, there are instances when we are more wrapped up in our own will than God's—or more concerned about what other people think than what our Divine Scheduler thinks. Ouch. One of my biggest challenges in learning to hurry less and worry less is to pray consistently about how I use my time. When I pray, I make better decisions and feel much more in tune with God's love and leadership.

Realize that taking on every good cause can wear you out and make you less effective at serving those you are called to serve. You may be asked to lead a small group at church, plan weekly refreshments for group meetings, help build a house for a family in need, or deliver meals to homebound people. At the same time you might be asked to help with a civic club fundraiser, attend a committee meeting, or volunteer your professional expertise to a class. These are all good causes, but you cannot do everything, no matter how good the cause.

Look for warning signs that you are overloading. Among the first warning signs is a schedule so jam-packed that you are unable to make a calm decision. You feel so stressed that you are not enjoying life, and you plow ahead when you know you should slow down. You snap at people you love and are rarely in the moment, instead thinking about what you *should* be doing or what you *have* to do in the next few days. Read Job 3:26 and see if you have ever felt like this: "I have no peace, no quietness; I have no rest, but only turmoil."

Another sign is that you have no time for prayer. Just as we must spend time to build relationships, we need to take time with God. A calming verse that brings me back to God is Psalm 46:10: "Be still, and know that I am God." We must still our busy selves and acknowledge God's presence. This stillness before God may come in a daily prayer time, in the early hours of the day before the busyness begins. It may come at church, sitting quietly and listening to a Bible passage or sermon or hymn. Sometimes it comes in nature—on a bench outdoors or in the park. Recently for me it has come when I look at the gorgeous hydrangeas that have bloomed so huge and blue that they take my breath away. They originally came to me as a tiny plant, a gift from the yard of a friend's grandmother who lived out in the country. I have not prayed for those hydrangeas, although I probably should have when they nearly died during a summer drought. But they are definitely an answered prayer in my heart.

Read and Depend on the Bible

Even if it seems impossible, set aside at least a few minutes of daily Bible study time, trying to build this into a habit. In trying to know and do the will of God, it is crucial you turn to the Bible for help—getting past the parts you may not understand and finding the message that God has for you. Answers abound when you turn to the Bible, even if you do not have much experience reading it. These ageless words can help you in myriad ways as you wrestle with everyday life.

My friends John and Terri Hill are co-pastors at Suntree United Methodist Church in Florida. They preached a series of sermons about favorite Scripture passages, verses that had shaped what they believe, think, and feel, and how they act. As Terri wrote in a church e-mail, "I don't know how people figure out who God is, what to pray, or what to believe if they don't read the Bible. At the same time I would be the first one to tell you that much in the Bible is not easy to understand. It was written many years ago by people in a very different culture.... And yet the basic issues are the same, the human needs are the same, the wisdom is eternal."

Understanding the stories of the Bible can help you make daily decisions and can provide a level of insight you will find nowhere else. You may be surprised when something you have read or heard in a Bible lesson percolates in your life, becoming an unexpected tool in a tough situation. In addition, the Bible contains the wonderful gospel of Christ—parables, instructions, examples. These stories about Jesus offer us a foundation of grace and give ideas on how to live in every situation.

Do not be intimidated by people who may have grown up attending church or who may have taken an in-depth Bible course. Jump right in! Take a class at church. Sit and listen. Learn how the Bible is organized. Tap into the power of its message, a power intended for your life. Pick out a verse each week and ponder it. Read the introductions to the books of the Bible that in many versions are found in the front of each book. These introductions provide a historical perspective and information about who wrote the book. Many Bibles have outlines of each chapter and describe themes and key messages. Review the scriptures your pastor preaches about. Pray for God's help in understanding how verses pertain to your daily life. Use a pencil or highlighter and mark scriptures. Make notes. Include the date. This will help you watch your inner life unfold. Though attending a class or Bible study may seem to *add* to your busy schedule, get ready. You will find yourself making decisions that open up more mind space.

Bible study will present new and encouraging thoughts, push aside negative thoughts, and clear out cobwebs. It opens up new places within you and helps you take your journey, step by step. It also helps you stay on the right path. As James 4:8 says: "Come near to God and he will come near to you."

Lean on God

Lean on God for rest even while searching for how you are to serve. "Come to me," Christ says, "all you who are weary and burdened, and I will give you rest. Take my yoke upon you and learn from me, for I am gentle and humble in heart, and you will find rest for your souls. For my yoke is easy and my burden is light" (Matthew 11:28-30).

Make space for learning to discern God's will for your life. You will be amazed at what opens for you along the way.

A Prayer for Your Journey

Dear Loving God, thank you for the many opportunities you send my way. I ask for wisdom as I consider how I am to spend my time and energy, that I will make good choices. Help me hurry less and worry less, so I might live more fully in you. In the holy name of Christ, amen.

Chapter Seven

HELP MY UNBELIEF

HOW TO GET ON THE RIGHT PATH

Encouraging Word: *God can do amazing things even when we are weak.*
Everyday Step: *Ask for forgiveness.*

"Be strong and courageous. Do not be terrified; do not be discouraged, for the LORD your God will be with you wherever you go." Joshua 1:9

*I*n 1980, two friends and I embarked on one of those two-week-see-lots-of-Europe tours. Being young and inexperienced, we stayed mostly with the group, quickly developing a comfort zone. However, also being young and adventursome, we took a few side jaunts, including a track meet at an Olympic stadium in Rome because one of us (not me) was dying to see star athlete Dwight Stones. The whole experience, including seeing Stones in his trademark Mickey Mouse shirt, was great fun—until we found ourselves stranded late at night in a dwindling crowd, unable to speak Italian and fairly certain we were done for.

In many ways, this escapade mirrors my own journey to know and do God's will. At times I have sought the comfort of the group, such as a church or class gathering where I felt at home, knew what was going on, and understood the lingo. At other times I have explored more, seeking new ideas and venturing out to stretch and grow. These explorations have always been exhilarating—with a little trepidation sprinkled in.

Sometimes it all seems so clear. And sometimes it is murky. I often wonder if God gets fed up with my floundering, when I ask God for help with some of the silliest things. I pray and try to do what I am called to do—and then I start wondering if I am really on track, using my gifts as God intended. I may start fretting about day-to-day concerns, such as scheduling and money and the logistics of life. Then I remember that God wants great things for me and understands my innermost being and *will guide me,* if I will only relax and let it happen.

When we make mistakes and bad choices, we may believe there is no turning back. This is no more true than if we slip up on a diet. ("Had one doughnut anyway, might as well have three. . . .") Maybe we are so tired that we do not want to make the effort to get on the right path. Fighting with the notion of having disappointed God can draw us right back to Murphy's Law: I *knew* I couldn't follow God's will for my life. Sometimes we feel unworthy or incapable of believing. But always our reassuring God shows tender mercy for us.

As Rob Weber, a United Methodist pastor and church leader, says, "Every time we come into God's presence, we are given the opportunity to begin again."

Moving Beyond Our Flaws

The Bible is full of people who messed up in big ways, only to serve God in greater ways later. Consider Moses, a giant of our faith. He tried to talk his way out of leading the Israelites to the promised land. He suggested that perhaps his brother or someone else could do the job. He made excuses. And God guided and used this same fellow to hand down the Ten Commandments and to teach us about daily faith—even though ultimately Moses disobeyed God and was not allowed into the promised land. Moses is a great example of someone who did great things for God despite his flaws.

Or there is Simon Peter, an impetuous fisherman who loved Christ, promised to fight to the death for him—and promptly denied knowing Jesus: "'Lord, I am ready to go with you to prison and to death.' Jesus answered, 'I tell you, Peter, before the rooster crows today, you will deny three times that you know me'" (Luke 22:33-34). And only hours later Peter did just that, looked up to see Jesus looking straight at him and "went outside and wept bitterly." Yet it was of this very human man, with all his doubts and flaws, that Jesus said: "And I tell you that you are Peter, and on this rock I will build my church, and the gates of Hades will not overcome it." And it was this man who became a leader in spreading the gospel after Christ's death, wrote two books of the Bible, and grew into a person who would do God's will, despite his flaws.

This list goes on and on, including Paul, who as Saul killed believers and then became a faithful and fervent believer himself. Then there was David, who gave us the Psalms and slayed the giant but also murdered a man and slept with someone else's wife. How must David have been feeling when he wrote Psalm 51, after many wrong decisions? "Have mercy on me, O God, according to your unfailing love; according to your great compassion blot out my transgressions. Wash away all my iniquity and cleanse me from my sin" (1-2). Have *you* ever felt like that?

Each of these people in the Bible remind us that God sees something in us that we cannot see and is willing to help us become more than we think possible.

If this were not enough, the Bible also overflows with stories of encouragement about people who were far from perfect but found God's will and love anyway.

One of these people is a father who brings his son to Christ to be healed, a child who has had some sort of terrible and disruptive illness for years. The father comes to Christ with an odd mix of hope and doubt, desperate, just like many of us. This man *does* believe and yet still struggles with unbelief. To my way of thinking, few people in the Bible capture the heart of those seeking God's guidance better than this father:

> "Jesus asked the boy's father, "How long has he been like this?"
>
> "From childhood," he answered. "It has often thrown him into fire or water to kill him. But if you can do anything, take pity on us and help us."
>
> " 'If you can'?" said Jesus. "Everything is possible for him who believes."
>
> Immediately the boy's father exclaimed, "I do believe; help me overcome my unbelief!" (Mark 9:23-24)

Another biblical character who is far from perfect is the Samaritan at the well, a woman who had a bad reputation and came to the town well at a different time than the other women. (Imagine someone known for doing bad things, judged by others, someone the other women did not want to associate with.) In John 4, we learn that Jesus was going through Samaria and, tired from his journey, sat down by the well while his disciples went into a nearby town to buy food. When Jesus asked the woman for a drink of water she was surprised, because usually in this situation a Jewish man would not talk to a Samaritan woman.

Jesus was kind to this woman and began to talk with her about the gift of "living water" and told her details about her life. She did not immediately grasp Christ's message, nor understand what it would mean in her daily life. In this conversation, however, the woman said she knew that a Messiah would come and explain everything to people. "Then Jesus declared, 'I who speak to you am he'" (John 4:26). Jesus used what could have been a very mundane encounter with an ordinary sinner to proclaim his lordship.

When the disciples returned, the woman left her water jar, went back to town, and told people to go to the well with her to see Jesus. "Many of the Samaritans from that town believed him because of the woman's testimony, 'He told me everything I ever did.' So when the Samaritans came to him, they urged him to stay with them and he stayed two days. And because of his words many more became believers" (John 4:39-41).

This is a remarkable story about how Christ can help us get back on the right path. The woman at the well had apparently made a series of wrong decisions in her life, resulting in serious relationship problems. Christ was willing to meet her where she was and talk with her about changing. Just like many of us, she was not quick to understand and hoped that Jesus' message would make her life easier. (She hoped Jesus' promise of living water meant that she would not have to go to the well each day for water.) As the visit unfolded, she accepted what he had to say and told others, inviting them back to meet Jesus. This testimony resulted in Christ extending his visit and in many becoming believers.

Encountering Christ in Daily Life

In the story of the woman at the well, what a marvelous image we get: Christ, weary from his journey, waiting for his helpers to get food and using the opportunity to talk with a woman about peace and mercy. Rich Varner, a part-time United Methodist pastor, says that Christ *really* enjoyed his work, and I think this story is a great example of that (and yet another reminder for us to find work we enjoy).

We do not know where we will encounter Jesus and receive help in our daily lives; it may very well be going about our daily routine, taking care of our chores, just as this woman was.

The people in the Bible sometimes got off track. But many of them made course corrections, coming to God to ask for help. They were willing to change. They went beyond a mixed-up place to a far better place. Such can be the case for us as we work to do the right things with our lives. When we acknowledge Christ's presence, he offers to help us find the right path and stay there.

I am reminded of how I feel when I visit New York City: I am intimidated by the tens of thousands of people rushing around Times Square, getting on and off the subway, jumping in and out of cabs, and pushing their way forward as though they have not one doubt about where they are headed, while I stand there trying to look confident and calm, wondering if I can cross the street without getting run over. Despite what we may sometimes think, other people have not been given a magical map that is being withheld from us. They, too, occasionally have to make a U-turn. Few have it completely figured out. For them, as for us, it is a daily journey, and the journey is sometimes very confusing. Picture yourself driving on a freeway, looking for the right exit, certain you are close and yet not knowing which way to go. First thing you know, you are somewhere you did not want to be and are completely off track—for the moment. Thankfully, these moments can be changed.

Here are some things to keep in mind when you stray:

Do not be too hard on yourself, beating yourself up for missteps or doubts. While you are called to do God's perfect will, you will find that our loving God understands when you fall short in trying to reach perfection. Keep working at it. You are forgiven when you err. You need not lose your hope when you lose your way.

Get some rest before deciding what to do. When you are worn out, it is very difficult to make a good decision. Try to increase your nightly sleep if you have been cutting it short. Take a few days of vacation from work to rest and renew.

Pray for wisdom, assessing what went wrong and why. The words of James tell us that God gives wisdom to those who ask and who believe: "If any of you lacks wisdom, he should ask God, who gives generously to all without finding fault, and it will be given to him" (James 1:5). This means not thinking secretly that you *knew* you would mess it up somehow. Instead, accept God's word and believe that you will be given wisdom to move forward in good ways.

Ask God for forgiveness, knowing your Creator is ready to help. God is not a trickster but a loving presence who wants good things for you.

Do not dread the future because of something that occurred in the past. Do not fear getting older and worry about what *could* happen. Our society is aging, so that means we are all getting older. Not to worry! The Bible is clear that God is with us throughout our lives. We can embrace transitions and look for new ways to serve God and live fully. Consider these words from Isaiah 46:4: "Even to your old age and gray hairs I am he, I am he who will sustain you. I have made you and I will carry you; I will sustain you and I will rescue you."

Seek out a community of believers, and ask for their help. The community might be a small group or class at church, or a pastor or spiritual director. A prayer partner is another resource. In such a relationship, you commit to pray with a trusted person on a regular basis.

We learn and grow as we move along. The mistakes of the past can become a foundation for doing it right next time. When I struggle to know if I am on the right path, I often turn to Philippians 1:6: "Being confident of this, that he who began a good work in you will carry it on to completion until the day of Christ Jesus." It's certain that I have not gotten things right every time, but God has an interest in my life. I have trusted Christ and have tried to do the right things at the right times. God will continue to work with what I have done, building on it until the job is completed—if I allow God to do so.

A Prayer for Your Journey

Heavenly God, thank you that you understand me. Thank you for helping me when I stumble and for leading me to you. Forgive me for what I have done wrong and help me know your will for me today. In the forgiving name of Christ, amen.

Chapter Eight

PAIN AND TRIUMPH

LEANING ON GOD IN HARD TIMES

Encouraging Word: *We can make it through hard times by remembering that God has a wonderful plan for us.*
Everyday Step: *Give thanks for what is going well in your life.*

"Peace I leave with you; my peace I give you. I do not give to you as the world gives. Do not let your hearts be troubled and do not be afraid." John 14:27

When I was a sophomore in college, the journalism department gave me the opportunity to go on an expense-paid trip to Philadelphia for a professional meeting. For a poor college student, this was an unexpected luxury. However, no sooner had I arrived in Pennsylvania than I received one of those calls you never want to get: my father, who had battled a chronic illness for years, was in critical condition, and I needed to hurry back. For a frightened young traveler, the trip home was excruciating and remains to this day a blur. Somehow I made it—to be greeted at the airport by one of my brothers telling me that Daddy had died minutes earlier.

Two years later, while a senior in college, I got another call. This one came to the cheap one-bedroom apartment I shared with two roommates, a ringing of the phone in the middle of the night that so often signals something bad. In a sleepy fog, I learned my mother had been taken to the hospital with a sudden illness. This call, from another brother, told me I needed to get home in a hurry. Mama was in the intensive care unit in my hometown more than two hundred miles away, the same spot where my dad had died two years earlier.

Those were the days before cell phones, and I was so afraid of what I would find when I arrived. However, my sweet, strong mother was still alive, on a respirator and only partly conscious. When I walked to her bedside, she roused a tiny bit, gave a slight (and very precious) smile, and slowly moved her fingers like scissors, commenting without words on my new, short haircut.

Within a few days, on a bitter November day, we stood in a rural Louisiana cemetery and buried her next to my father.

Just remembering this pain, three decades later, makes me sad. For months I struggled with this loss, my entire foundation shaken. I prayed. I cried. I wrote in my journal. I went to see the campus counselor. I wondered if the world would ever feel right again. Even now, as a grown woman with my own family and a full life, I miss my parents terribly and regret that they were taken so young.

These deaths and other tragedies through the years, for me and for the people I love, are a reminder that pain is a very real part of life. While it might seem nice to avoid it, we will encounter pain, probably more regularly than we would like. To pretend otherwise would be unfair and unwise. We often have no control over such events, no matter how good or how faithful we have been. Sometimes all we can do is cry out to God, allow ourselves to suffer, slowly regain our footing, and seek the wise aid of others to help heal the wounds.

In all situations we must choose how we will respond.

I think here of my friends Laura and Marty, who chose to face Marty's long battle with leukemia with faith and grace.

While no one thought their battle was easy, all those who knew them could see in their faces that they had called upon a peace that went beyond what the world could offer. When Marty died at age fifty, he inspired others to recall scriptures about trusting God in hard times. One verse he loved was Romans 8:18: "I consider that our present sufferings are not worth comparing with the glory that will be revealed in us." And his pastor chose another that told the story of Marty's life: "Therefore we do not lose heart.... So we fix our eyes not on what is seen, but on what is unseen. For what is seen is temporary, but what is unseen is eternal" (2 Corinthians 4:16, 18).

When we experience death and tragedy, we may find ourselves wondering how a loving God could allow such suffering. We may feel adrift, not certain about what we are to do. How could this possibly be part of God's will?

Months after Marty's death, Laura wrote of watching her husband's love for God grow and of the "deep and eternal purpose in the journey that we traveled."

She went on to write, "In the last year I have experienced such blessings from the Lord—in such incredible ways—so many answered prayers, from the very small and practical to the large and spiritual. The Holy Spirit has given me such a deep-seated peace and comfort that is so difficult to put into words.... It has become so clear to me that what our Christian life comes down to is a matter of our heart before God and our love for Him."

In my own life, I did not stop missing my parents or mourning the years I did not have them. I felt their absence at my wedding, at the birth of their youngest son's baby girl, and at church on Mother's Day. I did, however, come to realize that God was with me through all of this, bringing me out of a hard, sad place to a place of peace that defied explanation. God is with me now as I deal with the trials that I face as an adult. And God will be with me in whatever happens ahead.

When we are swamped by misery, we are not left alone and helpless. We can choose to call out to God and beg for the peace that passes understanding, to keep asking until we begin to feel a trickle of peace flow through us. When I am hit with a painful situation or tragedy, I often turn to a familiar New Testament passage that opens a door to healing: "Do not be anxious about anything, but in everything, by prayer and petition, with thanksgiving, present your requests to God. And the peace of God, which transcends all understanding, will guard your hearts and your minds in Christ Jesus" (Philippians 4:6-7).

These verses remind us not to worry, but to pray. They promise us that if we give thanks for all things and go to God with our needs, peace will settle over our hearts and our minds—a peace that goes well beyond what we can understand.

Reminders of Blessings

I have often had to work on being thankful in hard times. However, when I have paused and concentrated on the good, I have been swamped with reminders of blessings. Even during the dark days of the death of my parents, I was filled with gratitude to God—that I was privileged to have the parents I did, that my family has always stood together in good and bad times, that I had a good weekend at home with my dad in his last days, that I made it to see my mother before she died.

Each situation offers a chance for thankfulness, if we allow ourselves to see it. As I have gotten older, I have watched many of my friends care for their aging parents in very difficult situations, and I have been thankful my parents did not suffer for years. However, my friends in caregiving roles also offer thanks—that they have their parents in their lives and are able to care for them in old age. There is much to be thankful for, even though it may sometimes be hard to see.

In addition to situations beyond our control, there is the unhappiness we somehow bring on ourselves—the results of a bad decision we thought was good, a dumb choice we thought was smart. These situations can be especially painful when we were doing what we thought was God's will. In leading workshops and retreats, I regularly visit with people who are nearly paralyzed by choices they made that did not turn out the way they expected. Some of them have a haunted look in their eyes, wanting to trust God and move ahead but unsure of how to do so.

Throughout our lives we have been told to learn from our mistakes, but this is often difficult. Sometimes we can look back and see exactly where we went wrong—a decision in which we ignored our inner voice, a choice that was clearly destructive or unhealthy. At other times, though, we search and search and still cannot figure out where we went wrong. I think here of many people I have met through the years who thought they were marrying the person God had chosen for them, only to find they had married too soon or had ignored warning symptoms of alcoholism or were unaware of problems with handling money. Sometimes we are immature and make decisions out of ignorance, leading us to the wrong spouse or job or pastime.

Because we are human, we make mistakes. We sometimes get it wrong. This does not mean we will never get it right again or we are unable to make good choices. God is a forgiving, loving God who will help us all along the way.

Temporary Decisions, a Permanent God

Consider, too, that sometimes we make decisions that were right at the time but are no longer the best for us. It could be a job, for example, that was perfect for a season of time but no longer works with its long hours and stressful days. Or it could be a move that opened us to new people or new experiences, even though it did not turn out the way we expected.

Many of our decisions are temporary; we make them thinking they are forever but they are not. Others may work for years but then may need to be changed. As a journalist and newspaper executive for many years, I believed I was in the career that God wanted for me. I felt called to do the work. And when I began to hear a different call and to consider opening my own business, I struggled mightily, wondering if I had somehow gotten it wrong. Then I realized that I had gotten it right, and it was time for a change.

Even in situations where we have made mistakes, we can count on God's peace.

Never forget the power of the "Help me, God," prayer. Pick up the Bible and ask God to direct you to words to guide your life. "God is our refuge and strength, an ever-present help in trouble," we are told in Psalm 46:1. God is always with us when we are in trouble. Reminders of this are all around us.

Beyond the help of prayer and the Bible, turn to trusted people, such as a pastor or someone else at church. Do not be afraid to seek professional counseling; some situations require the objective eye and feedback of a professional.

Allow time for healing. Do not feel as though you must rush into a new situation or fix everything all at once. Ponder.

Through bad times, always ask God's forgiveness for choices that brought pain or actions that were wrong. God forgives us when we make mistakes, and steadies us when we stumble. And we must learn to forgive ourselves, to believe we have done the best we can do, and to ask for guidance for the best next step.

Need a reminder of how much God loves you? "How great is the love the Father has lavished on us, that we should be called children of God! And that is what we are!" (1 John 3:1). Or perhaps you will choose another verse that reminds you that God loves you and walks with you each day. For mighty comfort, soak up Psalm 103:1-5: "Praise the LORD, O my soul; all my inmost being, praise his holy name. Praise the LORD, O my soul, and forget not all his benefits— who forgives all your sins and heals all your diseases, who redeems your life from the pit and crowns you with love and compassion, who satisfies your desires with good things so that your youth is renewed like the eagle's."

Developing a deep awareness of God in our lives also helps us when things are going exceedingly well. When I was a young editor in a small newsroom, we hired an outstanding reporter who always seemed to know what to do. I found myself spending less time with him and trying to help other staff members, who seemed to be struggling. After a few months, the new reporter came to me asking for more feedback and guidance—reminding me that even when people seem to have it all together, they still need help. The same is true in our lives.

We may tend to neglect God when things are going well, or we may forget to offer ongoing thanks and to ask for guidance to make good decisions. When something good happens, we may feel as though we accomplished it on our own, through our intelligence or hard work. The reality is that, in good and bad, we must lean on God, praying, offering thanks, seeking wisdom and trust.

My life has been flooded with happy, sunny days. And there have been gray November cemetery days too. The divine will is in place for each of these. Divine gifts are also in place—the peace of Christ that goes beyond what the world can offer, and a stillness that keeps my heart from being troubled and afraid.

A Prayer for Your Journey

Dear Holy Lord, thank you for walking with me during the dark days. Thank you for your assurance that you are with me always, even when life seems hard. Please help me trust in you and follow your guidance. Forgive me when I falter. In the healing name of Christ, amen.

Chapter Nine

ALIVE IN CHRIST

GUIDELINES FOR HAPPINESS

Encouraging Word: *God will keep you strong each day.*
Everyday Step: *Make choices that support your priorities.*

*" 'Love the Lord your God with all your heart and with all
your soul and with all your mind. This is the first and
greatest commandment. And the second is like it: Love
your neighbor as yourself.' " Matthew 22:37-39*

One of the first how-to books I ever bought was an exer-
cise guide. The book had a title that involved being lazy and
having a much better body in thirty days. It started my deep
commitment to fitness and began a lifelong fascination with
magazine articles, books, and television programs that
would give me tips on how to do something better, easier,
more quickly. As I examine my own life and observe those of
others, I realize that most people want a simple how-to list
for happiness. This often includes the easiest way to make
more money, lose more weight, and find true love.

Moving forward in the way God wants us to is an ongoing process, not some quick fix that occurs in thirty days or
less. However, it is also astonishingly simple because it cen-
ters around one thing: the great love of Christ, which comes
wrapped in the abundant grace that God offers. The teachings of Christ provide guidelines for happiness, and God's
law of grace far surpasses Murphy's Law.

As we say at the church I attend, *grace happens.*

Jesus understands our searching hearts: "I tell you the truth, my Father will give you whatever you ask in my name.... Your joy will be complete" (John 16:23-24). Choose to trust God, even in the shaky times, and call upon the promise in 1 Corinthians 1:8: "He will keep you strong to the end."

To live with Christ's love at our center requires knowing more about Christ, being aware of what makes us happy and why, and exploring ways to put aside destructive or distracting things on our journey. As we do these things, the Spirit of the living God infuses us. This happens often to our great surprise and without our complete understanding. The Bible says that God's words are written not on paper but on our hearts, and this means our lives become a how-to guide in and of themselves.

When I was a child, I walked to the altar of Parkview Baptist Church, in a sanctuary where the sun came through the stained glass windows in an almost holy way. Even though I was young and certainly not wise, I wanted to accept Christ's grace and to tell the world that I had faith in Jesus. I recall the words of "Softly and Tenderly Jesus Is Calling" being sung and, the evening of my baptism, stepping into a tank of water and being weighed down with a soggy white robe. When I came up, splashing and gasping for air, I had a feeling of being alive in Christ. The words of 2 Corinthians 5:17 were somehow written on my heart: "Therefore, if anyone is in Christ, he is a new creation; the old has gone, the new has come!"

In those same days, though, I was also playing tag on the wide walkway out front, between the giant oaks, and learning about foreign countries in mission classes. I had made a big first step, but I certainly had a long way to go. When I think about it now, I realize I had come to Christ as a child, trusting, but this was only the beginning of the adventure of a life that would be blessed greatly.

As the years unfolded, I needed to learn and grow, from the Bible, from other books, from leaders, from friends who had faith. The ongoing steps of following would be my challenge. Perhaps you have experienced this in your own life, having come to Christ early in life or maybe beginning to develop faith as an adult. You may even now be taking steps toward a decision that will change your life. Maturing, I realized that I could delight in this new life in Christ and take the steps boldly and with joy—or I could succumb to Murphy's Law, fret and fear, and never truly be alive in Christ. Moving forward, we can know that no matter what we do, God will help us: "For God's gifts and his call are irrevocable" (Romans 11:29).

What Next?

Throughout my journey, I have found myself thankful for all the blessings God has given me—and often wondering what I need to do next. I regret the moments I have squandered because I was trying so hard to make it work *my* way. And I am thrilled with the moments when I have embraced the simplicity of true grace. Our relationship with Christ can be one that grows and helps us tap into the power of God. As believers, trying to become the people God wants us to be, we are children of God. This is not some distant relationship, like the wife of your third cousin on your mom's side. This is a close connection: "God has made you also an heir" (Galatians 4:7). This means that God's will includes us. We inherit this extraordinary life in Christ. If you have ever inherited anything, even something small from a friend or relative, you know the special feeling of excitement that arises. Considering this verse in that light shows how special the relationship with Jesus is.

To live fully, trying our best to follow God and to savor the blessings we have been given, is to be aware of God's promises and presence, of answered prayer, of generous blessings and people God puts on our path. My friend Carol uses the word "available" in her life to remind her to be accessible and useful to someone God wants her to serve at any given moment. I believe this idea captures how we are to live—to be *available* to do what God is calling us to do.

Basic principles help develop a road map for happiness. They can be summed up in only three sentences: *Love God with all your heart. Love your neighbor. Love yourself.*

But these simple sentences require commitment and discipline. They may be tough to put into practice. Our joy comes in learning how the sentences are reflected in our daily lives, how they shape us as we get out of bed each day and move through the challenges of life—even on Mondays.

Look around at people who try to live by these words and use them as a model. As I was finishing this book, for example, a longtime family friend died, a man who had been key in my childhood church life. In a tribute, his family wrote: "He derived his greatest happiness not from his own personal entertainment, but from playing his role in God's Grand Scheme, which included caring for his family and others." The man was alive in Christ throughout his career as a doctor, on his many beloved fishing trips, and in the commitment he made to the local church. During the last months of his life, when he was sick, he offered this prayer daily: "We know not the future, but we place it in your hands." He lived fully and richly—because he knew God had a better plan for him.

To form a life that is alive, full of wonder and delight, consider these approaches:

Start with the teachings of Jesus. Believe in Christ as your savior and learn about his life and the lessons he taught so profoundly and simply. Understand that you have what you need in this gift of grace, enough for whatever you are meant to do: "My grace is sufficient for you, for my power is made perfect in weakness" (2 Corinthians 12:9). What an amazing concept that God's power is made *perfect* in our weakness.

Live with a purpose. Set goals, listening for clues from God for what to do in each situation. This does not mean overplanning, but it does mean knowing what you want your life to look like, including steps you might take to be alive in Christ, full of life and hope. (Consider this image from 1 Corinthians 9:26: "Therefore I do not run like a man running aimlessly; I do not fight like a man beating the air.")

Show kindness to others, living the Golden Rule: "So in everything, do to others what you would have them do to you" (Matthew 7:12). My mother's version of the Golden Rule has guided me through life: "You be nice to them, and they'll be nice to you." Lately I have been watching birds in my backyard annoy other birds, relentlessly heckling their prey, flying too close, swooping aggressively. They remind me of people who target others for trouble and make life difficult. The world needs kind people. Be one.

Be thankful for the many good things God does for you, blessings that make your life sweeter and more enjoyable. I am in awe of God and what we have, even when circumstances seem rocky. God's love and provision and care and grace and forgiveness surround each of us if we will reach out and ask. We are to use these gifts to help others, to show God's glory to others, to make this tired, hurting world a better place. We are to relish the gifts and hold them near as precious and life-giving. "He performs wonders that cannot be fathomed, miracles that cannot be counted" (Job 9:10).

Be willing to believe that things work out for the best. A *willingness* to believe comes before the actual believing. Ellen, a friend and United Methodist pastor, tells a great story about mountain climbing on a Boy Scout trip with her son. The challenge *seemed* like a good idea on the way up, but then she became anxious as she rappelled down. She was determined, though, not to give up. She stayed connected to the person at the bottom, believing, even in fear, that she would make it. Had she lost her nerve, she could have taken a nearby trail but would have missed an exhilarating experience. Ellen learned that as we open ourselves to changes in attitudes and actions, we can begin to follow God more consistently. Remember Psalm 68:19: "Praise be to the Lord, to God our Savior, who *daily* bears our burdens" (italics added).

Expect the best, not the worst. A member of my small group at church, a quiet carpenter, says that as children of God we are all called according to God's purpose, and therefore we are assured all will work out for good. This goes well beyond the cliché of patting you on the hand and telling you something was "meant to be." It does not mean that our lives are always going to be just the way we want them to be. We may have our hearts broken or our feelings bruised or our confidence shaken at times, but the Lord of the universe goes with us through every situation. Remember: "And we know that in all things God works for the good of those who love him, who have been called according to his purpose" (Romans 8:28).

Need further assurance? Read on in Romans for a breathtaking promise. "Neither death nor life, neither angels nor demons, neither the present nor the future, nor any powers, neither height nor depth, nor anything else in all creation, will be able to separate us from the love of God that is in Christ Jesus our Lord" (Romans 8:38-39). Having a tough time feeling true happiness? Tape this passage to your mirror, your computer, your refrigerator door—and write it on your heart.

Keep seeking God's answers and trying to become stronger in your faith. Read your Bible and make notes. In my late forties, I read with new eyes these words in Philippians 2:12-13: "Continue to work out your salvation with fear and trembling, for it is God who works in you to will and to act according to his good purpose." While it might seem odd that I wrote "Awesome!" in the margins of my Bible, I find comfort in knowing that God has given me permission to struggle and work out questions in my life with fear and trembling.

Know that God watches over you all the time. "I lift up my eyes to the hills—where does my help come from? My help comes from the LORD, the Maker of heaven and earth. He will not let your foot slip—he who watches over you will not slumber.... The LORD will keep you from all harm—he will watch over your life; the LORD will watch over your coming and going both now and forevermore" (Psalm 121:1-3, 7, 8).

Opt for Happiness

We are not to go through life letting Murphy dictate our responses. We are reminded again and again that "because of his great love for us, God, who is rich in mercy, made us alive with Christ" (Ephesians 2:4-5).

As you try on this idea to see how it fits in your life, look at what might be distracting you or what might be destructive. Examine the daily choices you make. Are they in keeping with what you truly believe? Are they in sync with how you believe God wants you to live? Begin to be aware of what brings you unhappiness, so you can set that aside to opt for happiness. As you move through each day, you'll find that possibilities abound for joyful moments. We are not like children bouncing around in an inflatable house, hitting the sides, falling down and staggering to our feet, confined and limited. God's plan liberates us: "I run in the path of your commands, for you have set my heart free.... Direct me in the path of your commands, for there I find delight" (Psalm 119: 32, 35).

May you be alive in Christ as you seek and do God's will.

A Prayer for Your Journey

Dear God, thank you for grace and for Jesus Christ. Help me learn more about loving you above all and about loving myself and others. Help me show kindness to those around me and move through my daily life with mercy. In the sweet name of Christ, amen.

Chapter Ten

A CONTENTED HEART

SAVORING THE JOURNEY

Encouraging Word: *You can learn to be content.*
Everyday Step: *Decide what you would most like God to do for you.*

"To him who is able to keep you from falling and to present you before his glorious presence without fault and with great joy—to the only God our Savior be glory, majesty, power and authority, through Jesus Christ our Lord, before all ages, now and forevermore! Amen." Jude 24-25

*F*lying home recently from a business trip, I found myself uneasy about the weather. I was on a small, bumpy jet with huge thunderheads in the distance and thick clouds obscuring any view of the ground. As the plane began to descend, I clinched the arms of the seat, took a deep breath, and whispered a prayer. Then I glanced out the window, and a stunningly clear view of my hometown in north Louisiana appeared just below the clouds—the skyline downtown, the very red Red River, the lake, the neighborhoods I knew so well. Although I had flown in and out of that airport dozens of times, I could not remember ever having such a great view. I could see every detail. Contrasted with the clouds and bad weather, it was an especially startling blessing.

That clear vision, with peace after turbulence, is what contentment looks like to me.

When we are contented, our heart and soul experience an odd mix of soaring and calm, with a sense that no matter what happens, all will be well. In life, as on that flight, the sense of tranquility and delight often comes on the heels of difficult situations. We are zooming through life on a bumpy ride, holding on tight and hoping for the best, unable to see what is just ahead. And suddenly we break through and see what was beneath those clouds all along—a beautiful view of our life, spread out, with things working out just as they should.

As our life moves along, we want to get it right. We do not want to throw away the days we have been given or waste the joys that could have been ours. We long to hear God tell us one day that we have lived and served well, been good and faithful. Yet so often we live in turbulence, expecting the worst to happen, reacting to situations that come our way, tight-knuckled and unable to relax and enjoy the day. Murphy's Law can steal our contentment when this happens, and before we know it, the days have zipped by and we have slipped into a dull routine that is uncertain and sometimes unhappy.

Consider instead living with contentment. It unfolds as we learn and grow and come to appreciate each day for the wonder it brings. As we seek God's will for our lives, we do not have to get everything perfect to feel contented. If we allow ourselves, we can experience contentment simply by knowing that we are *trying* to discover and do God's will. In John 10:10, Christ told us he came that we might have abundant life. Murphy's Law is the antithesis of that abundance; it shrinks our joy and steals our contentment. Instead of counting our blessings, we expect the worst and affirm it when it happens: "I *knew* that was too good to be true."

We are to savor the abundance of our daily journey, and God's will is part of that fullness.

Minor Details, Major Distractions

Do not let distractions erode your contentment. In my life, I have spent far too little time taking advantage of contentment. I have overplanned the present, fretted about the future, and let precious moments slip away from me, preoccupied with minor details that did not matter. I think here of a familiar character in the New Testament, Martha.

Martha and her sister Mary loved Christ and were devoted followers. Martha was given the blessing of Christ's presence in her home but used some of her time to complain that her sister was not helpful enough. When Jesus paid a visit, Mary sat at Christ's feet listening to what he said. "But Martha was distracted by all the preparations that had to be made" (Luke 10:40). Christ told her that she was upset about the wrong things. I can easily see myself doing something similar, scurrying around, checking items off my to-do list, and forgetting to enjoy and be content in that incredible visit with Christ.

Contentment can come not only when things are going well but also when we deal with the daily floods that threaten to drown us. Assurance can come in knowing that we have the ear of God, no matter how great our problems. Often we feel like the Psalmist: "Save me, O God, for the waters have come up to my neck. I sink in the miry depths, where there is no foothold" (Psalm 69:1-2).

We can learn to respond to situations in love instead of frustration or anger. When we act out of love, our hearts often relax. If we weave "do unto others" into this, we feel better about those we encounter each day and more contented in how relationships and situations play out.

We can begin to shape our lives by pausing to consider how contentment looks. For most, contentment is a sense that all is well and that we have a peace that goes beyond the moment. It usually requires slowing down a bit (hurry less!) and it also means giving up fretting (worry less!). We trust that things will turn out good. Contentment does not include trying to control every situation or constantly wishing for something we don't have—more money, a different relationship, another job. We may want or even need those things. But we must learn to be content within ourselves, whatever the situation in our lives.

The apostle Paul understood that contentment would come not because everything was always perfect but because we could draw on a deeper source of joy. In his familiar words in Philippians 4:11-13, he wrote: "I have learned to be content whatever the circumstances. I know what it is to be in need, and I know what it is to have plenty. I have learned the secret of being content in any and every situation, whether well fed or hungry, whether living in plenty or in want. I can do everything through him who gives me strength."

Contentment probably did not come easily to Paul. He was somewhat of a control freak and had high expectations of his life and of the people he met, both before and after his conversion. He learned to find contentment by looking at the details of his daily life (being "content in any and every situation") and turning to Christ for strength. There was nothing stingy about it: "I can do *everything* through him who gives me strength." This is not something you are either born with or not. Resist the tendency to let other people tell you what you are or are not and can or cannot do—"Oh, he's just a negative person" or "She won't be able to make it in that job." Contentment is available to each of us in our everyday lives. Like Paul, we can *learn* to be contented. We can learn it through useful stories in the Bible, through prayer and the advice of others, and most of all through the strength we find in Christ.

Seeing Life with New Eyes

Practicing contentment is not easy for most of us; it is a skill that requires patience (often in short supply), gratitude, and trust in God. We can learn to enjoy watching God's great plan unfold. Through the years I have come to believe that true contentment comes as we see more clearly what we are to be doing and as we try our best to do it. We are like the blind beggar in Luke 18, a character whose story has affected me powerfully these past few years. Imagine this scene in your mind, something that could have been right out of a movie:

A blind man sits by the road, begging. He hears the commotion of a crowd and asks what is going on. People tell him that Jesus is passing by, and he begins to call out for mercy from Christ. Instead of helping the man, people tell him to be quiet. You can almost hear their embarrassed scolding. He shouts even more. The man is obviously desperate, and yet we sense that he is also hopeful. He believes there is a better plan for his life; he is *not* sitting there thinking that Christ will probably never come by to help him.

Now the story takes a twist.

Jesus stops and orders that the man be brought to him. I think of the crowd jostling around Jesus and of the man being led to Christ, believing, hoping, unable to see, unsure of what will happen next. As the man gets close, Christ asks one of my favorite questions in the Bible: "What do you want me to do for you?" (Luke 18:41).

The man knows what he needs from Jesus and says it clearly and forthrightly: " 'Lord, I want to see,' he replied" (verse 41).

Jesus immediately does what the man wants: "Receive your sight; your faith has healed you" (verse 42).

When I stray from the happiness God has in mind for me, it is often because I am not clear about what to do and when. I have lost my "soul sight." If I had encountered Christ on that road, I might have asked for clarity in my life—knowing God's will and how I am to live that will. To me, that is the essence of contentment. I want to encounter Christ regularly and to use the lessons I have learned from the blind man:

- **Be aware.** As the beggar sat by the road, he was aware, listening and willing to ask others what was going on. He was observant, even though he was blind.
- **Ask for help.** The beggar cried out to Jesus, refusing to be discouraged by those who were trying to silence him. He was desperate and willing to do what needed to be done.
- **Be persistent.** The beggar yelled repeatedly for mercy. He would not sit back quietly and let the opportunity for blessing pass him by.
- **Trust in Christ.** When Jesus asked *the question* ("What do you want me to do for you?"), the beggar knew what he needed most, and he asked for it with faith. ("Lord, I want to see.") He trusted that if he could get Christ's attention, Christ would heal him.
- **Praise God.** When the beggar received his sight, he followed Jesus and praised God. And because of what happened in his life, those around him praised God too. Already he was using his blessings to be a grateful follower.

What Do You Need from Christ?

Through the years I have begged God for this and that. I have struggled to know what to do, thrashing around like a young child just learning to swim, afraid to let go of the side of the pool but yearning to go deeper. And then I have remembered the simple question that Christ still asks us today: "What do you want me to do for you?"

Just reading this question ignites a spark of hope and contentment deep within. It's not that I have it all figured out and do it right every day. It's not that I am flawless or can go through life like a robot with a painted smile on my face. The contentment comes from realizing that God wants good things in my life and is willing to meet my needs. It seeps into my heart and soul, and I long to live peacefully and not fearfully. It erases Murphy's Law and replaces it with the belief that things are going to work out. I have to do my part: be present, observe, ask Christ for help, trust. And then Christ, without fail, will do his.

Christ Is Coming Our Way

Sometimes contentment washes over us, eliciting a heart-felt thank-you to God for allowing us to move beyond our own small-mindedness. It often comes in small, unexpected moments when we are suddenly aware of the greatness of life, the way I saw the clear sky and city view as I returned home that day in a storm. Sometimes the moment comes when we are out of our routine and realize that God's hand has been guiding us longer than we realized. I recall an early-morning jog on the campus of Baylor University when I was visiting Waco on a business trip. The sun was rising, a huge moon was setting, and I was enjoying happy memories of my time there as a student. The joy I felt went beyond the moment and reminded me of how much I have been given, how God continues to help me grow, and how astonishing life is. Look for moments such as these. Soak up God's guidance like a sponge. Watch your heart swell with contentment.

Consider the power of God in your own life. Appreciate the wonder. Draw on the strength that is so much more than you can imagine. Rather than make a list of what has irritated or frustrated or disappointed you, train yourself to count your blessings.

Hoyt Byrum, a Presbyterian pastor and dear friend, says: "To be content, be thankful." If we can live by this thought, we can soar.

Start each day with a prayer of gratitude for all that is working in your life and all that will go right this day. "But be sure to fear the LORD and serve him faithfully with all your heart; consider what great things he has done for you" (1 Samuel 12:24).

Move forward with the certainty that Christ will guide you as you walk down the road of your daily life and that he stands willing to provide what you need. Knowing this, feel contentment seep into your very soul. God's plan ... at work ... in you.

Whatever can go wrong, God can make right. Goodbye, Murphy's Law.

A Prayer for Your Journey

Dear God, thank you for giving me the ability to rest in you. Help me be content with my life today, give thanks for the good, and consider changes I might need to make. Please, Lord, help me know your awesome peace and share it with those I encounter today. In the powerful name of Christ, amen.

STUDY GUIDE FOR INDIVIDUALS AND GROUPS

"Call to me and I will answer you and tell you great and unsearchable things you do not know." Jeremiah 33:3

Goodbye, *Murphy's Law* can be used by individuals or groups for in-depth study, to go deeper in learning about God's will and living with hope. This study guide is intended to help readers learn how to seek and do God's will in their daily lives.

Using the book's ten chapters as an outline, the guide provides for each chapter:
- a reflection on the Scripture
- a key point to consider
- study questions
- a step to take in the week ahead

With Scripture passages woven through the text, this study can help readers learn more about the Bible and how to incorporate biblical teachings into everyday life. Individuals can answer the questions in a journal or notebook during quiet time. Groups can use them to shape conversation.

The study invites participation, but it also focuses on each individual's journey and is suited for a diverse group. Each of us is uniquely created, and we are at different places in our lives. This means that responses are very personal and may vary greatly. Each person is special, and there are no right or wrong answers. This study can help a small group or Sunday school class develop spiritually and in relationship to one another. It can help individuals discover the next steps on their journey.

Suggestions for Individual Study

I have found personal study time to be immensely useful and very hard to maintain. Using a book as a guide has been helpful, as I hope this book will help you. You may come to know God better by developing or refining the habit of prayer, reflection, and Bible study. Stepping back from your daily routine regularly is part of this process.

Use the study questions in the guide to direct your quiet time. Consider using a journal or notebook as you move through the book, jotting down your ideas and pondering how God might be speaking to you each day. A journal can be a very helpful tool as you sort out your thoughts. You can also list prayer requests, jot down things you are thankful for, and write prayers.

Many of us bog down during individual study time for a variety of reasons. The most common reason is that it's hard to find study time in our busy, noisy lives. I encourage you to set aside time to read a chapter of the book and then to reflect upon it. You might allow a little time every day or several days a week, building it into your schedule. As a morning person, I like to greet the day with quiet time. However, night owls may prefer to plan for time in the evening. Find a spot where you can have privacy and quiet—a time and place where you are less likely to be interrupted.

If you get off track, pray about it and try again. God understands your life and will guide you.

Start or Join a Small Group

Becoming part of a community of strugglers, believers, and people who want to know and love God is a joyful experience. Such a group can add richness to your life, providing you with people from whom you can learn and grow—and have fun with. These groups often become like a loving family, helping one another in tough times and celebrating together in good times. While group meetings do not replace individual quiet time, they add a new perspective to study.

How do you find such a group? If you attend church, ask at the office or take a look at the website. If you have not found a church to call home, ask friends or co-workers. Most groups are happy to have guests from outside the congregation.

These groups come in all forms. Some meet on Sunday mornings and are similar to Sunday school classes that you might remember from childhood. Others meet in the evening. Some share teaching responsibilities, so you will hear the viewpoints of a variety of people. Others have one leader, with participation from class members. In nearly all cases, groups are receptive to your individual style, whether you like to talk or prefer to sit back quietly, whether you grew up in church or have not been to church in years.

If you have been involved in a church or Bible study, you might want to consider *starting* a new small group. Pray about this and ask God to send the right people, and you will be amazed at how your group might form. Often a church staff member will know of people interested in a new group, and organizing it can be an astonishing ministry. This is a good way to serve and use such gifts as teaching, leadership, and hospitality.

Remember: You do not have to be a preacher or Bible scholar to lead a small group. You simply have to help pull the group together, encourage others, and be yourself. If you feel called to lead a group, study for each class. Jot down an agenda for the meeting to keep you on track, and use notes as needed. Notify members where you will meet and when. Encourage group participation, but do not try to force anyone to talk. Pray each week for an awareness of God's presence in the midst of your group.

One of your key jobs will be to create a place where people can talk candidly about life and learn about their journey. This is an awesome role and can help you serve God in a meaningful way.

Suggestions for Group Leaders

The study can last from five to ten weeks, focusing on one or two chapters a meeting. Each session can last from one hour to an hour-and-a-half, depending on the amount of time you allow for discussion. Participants should read the chapters in advance to prepare for the discussion and to think about how God is speaking in their lives.

To get your room ready, add touches to make it more personal and comfortable. Consider a candle, for example, and perhaps a cross or flowers or an item symbolic of the week's discussion. You might ask group members to help with such items, making this a participatory activity.

Be on hand early to greet members and welcome visitors. Some groups enjoy taking turns bringing snacks or a light meal. This practice can help build a close spirit in the group and help newcomers relax as the group gathers.

Open each session with prayer, asking for God's presence in the discussion. Invite group discussion all along the way, but do not try to force anyone to share. As the weeks unfold, you will likely find that members are more eager to open up. Remind your group that class discussions are confidential. Make sure each person has pen and paper.

A sample session:

- Open with prayer and have casual conversation with your group, chatting as participants settle.
- Direct participants to "Going a Step Further" below, using this as an outline for the class.
- Focus on the written scripture at the beginning of each chapter as the group starts.
- Begin the discussion with the "key point to consider."
- Lead the group in answering and discussing the study questions.
- Ask individuals to choose a step they will take during the coming week and invite them to reflect on their thoughts during the course of the week.
- Assign chapters to be read before the next meeting.
- End the session with prayer requests and a prayer for God's guidance for each person as all of you seek to know and do the Lord's will.

Going a Step Further: Study Questions for Groups or Individuals

After reading each chapter and reflecting on the scripture, turn to the "key point to consider" and what it means in your life. Use the study questions to take you a step further and help you sense how God is leading. You are a special individual, unlike anyone else in the world. God wants to do great things in your life, and these things may be completely different for each person. As you use the following guide, ask yourself what God's will is for *your* life. Pray about your answers, and let them shape your life.

1. The Key
How God's plan can change our lives

Reflection on Romans 12:2. What does this verse mean in your life?

Key point to consider. Knowing God's will does not usually come with a burning bush or handwriting on the wall. Instead, it is like any other ability we want to develop: we must pray, focus on it, learn specific skills, and practice. This all happens by moving forward one step at a time.

Study questions
- Chapter 1 points out that many people believe whatever can go wrong will go wrong. What evidence of this do you see in your life?
- How might you change this thinking to expect good things to happen?
- What seems to be going right in your life?
- What might need changing in your life?
- Have you ever had a time when you felt distant from God? What are some steps you might take to build closeness with God?

A step you might take in the week ahead to know God's will. (Individual to supply)

2. Take Hope
God wants good things for your life

Reflection on 1 Corinthians 2:9. What does this verse mean in your life?

Key point to consider. God has created us to live with hope at the core of our being—with a way of thinking that anticipates rather than dreads.

Study questions
- Chapter 2 mentions the importance of hope in our daily lives. In what ways are you hopeful in your life?
- What draws you away from being hopeful?
- How might you build hope in your daily life?
- How can hope help you worry less?
- Make a list of things that went right in your life this past week.

A step you might take in the week ahead to be more hopeful. (Individual to supply)

3. God's Workmanship
Steps to becoming the person you were created to be

Reflection on Psalm 90:17. What does this verse mean in your life?

Key point to consider. The power of God resides in each of us, unique and wonderful. God has a job for us to do—and that job is woven into each of us. We can do something that no one else can do.

111

Study questions
- Chapter 3 says we are equipped to do something special with our lives. Why is this idea sometimes tough to follow? In what ways have you balked at God's guidance?
- In what ways have you sensed God's "equipping" in your own life?
- What gives you energy?
- What drains your energy?
- How might you allow God to guide your work life more completely?

A step you might take in the week ahead to enjoy work or volunteer activities more fully. (Individual to supply)

4. Talking with God, Listening to God
How prayer can help

Reflection on 1 John 5:14. What does this verse mean in your life?

Key point to consider. God welcomes our prayers and invites us to ask for guidance and for what we need. Building a prayer life is a key step in learning how to know and do God's will.

Study questions
- Chapter 4 reminds us of God's promises to answer our prayers. In what ways do you find it easy to go to God in prayer, and in what ways do you find it difficult?
- How has God shown you the power of prayer in your life?
- Consider people you enjoy being with in your daily life.

How do you build those relationships? How might you use those same approaches to build a closer relationship with God?

• List something you are thankful for and something you are concerned about. Offer those to God in prayer.

A step you might take in the week ahead to develop a regular prayer time. (Individual to supply)

5. Impatient for Change
How to wait for God's guidance

Reflection on Psalm 40:1. What does this verse mean in your life?

Key point to consider. Waiting for God's guidance is important. We need to learn to move beyond our impatience and use waiting as an opportunity for renewal.

Study questions
• Chapter 5 says God understands our weaknesses and can help us learn to wait. Why is waiting so difficult?
• In what areas of your life do you need God's help in learning to wait?
• As we wait, we must learn to trust God with our daily lives. How have you seen God's timing play out in your life?
• As you consider future decisions in your life, what preparations or planning might you need to do?
• How might you use times of waiting as a source of renewal?

A step you might take in the week ahead to wait more patiently. (Individual to supply)

6. Do Less, Be More
Opening up space for God's help

Reflection on Psalm 131:2. What does this verse mean in your life?

Key point to consider. When we get too busy, it is easy to become wrapped up in our own will. If we are to do God's will and live fully, we must learn to clear out room for God, to do less and be more.

Study questions
- Chapter 6 says that learning to prioritize activities and making good choices about our schedule is a spiritual discipline. What activities in your life might need a second look?
- What activities do you most enjoy?
- Many people have a difficult time saying no. List three ways to say no when you believe a request is not right for your life.
- Christ regularly stepped back from noisy crowds. What time during the week might you use to step back and listen for God's guidance?
- What is something special that you want to make time to do?

A step you might take in the week ahead to open up space in your life. (Individual to supply)

7. Help My Unbelief
How to get on the right path

Reflection on Joshua 1:9. What does this verse mean in your life?

Key point to consider. The Bible is full of people who messed up in big ways, only to serve God in greater ways later. We, too, can redirect our steps and be forgiven when we stray from God's path.

Study questions
- Chapter 7 suggests that every time we come into God's presence, we are given the opportunity to begin again. In what ways do you need a fresh start?
- A father brought his son to Jesus for healing and said, "I do believe; help me overcome my unbelief!" Consider times in your life when you have felt the same way. What caused this mix of feelings?
- Think of a time when you needed the forgiveness of God in a special way. Ask God to forgive you and help you move ahead.
- In what areas of your life do you need wisdom to move forward?
- Name three great decisions you have made in your life.

A step you might take in the week ahead to put past mistakes behind you. (Individual to supply)

8. Pain and Triumph
Leaning on God in hard times

Reflection on John 14:27. What does this verse mean in your life?

Key point to consider. When hard times hit, we are not alone and helpless. We can call out to God and receive the peace that passes understanding.

Study questions
- Chapter 8 reminds us that life can be painful at times and that we may struggle to understand God's will. Describe a time when you needed assurance that God was with you.
- Describe a time when things worked out well, even though you thought they might not.
- In what areas of your life might you need healing and the peace of God which passes understanding?
- Sometimes we neglect God when things are going well. Name five things you give special thanks for in your life, things that have gone very well.
- What helpful lesson have you learned from a painful time in the past?

A step you might take in the week ahead to be more open to God's peace. (Individual to supply)

9. Alive in Christ
Guidelines for happiness

Reflection on Matthew 22:37-39. What do these verses mean in your life?

Key point to consider. We are children of God, and our relationship with Christ is to be one that grows and helps us connect with the power of God.

Study questions
- Chapter 9 mentions that the grace of God and the teachings of Christ provide guidelines for happiness. In what ways have you felt "grace happen" in your own life?

- What does true happiness mean to you? What changes might you need to make in your daily life in order to be happier?
- Sometimes others irritate us, and it is difficult to practice the Golden Rule. Name three people who need your kindness or love.
- Name two or three lessons of Christ that can help you in your daily life.
- What distractions threaten to separate you from God's love in your daily life?

A step you might take in the week ahead to love others more completely. (Individual to supply)

10. A Contented Heart
Savoring the journey

Reflection on Jude 24-25. What do these verses mean in your life?

Key point to consider. Contentment unfolds as we learn and grow and come to appreciate each day for the wonder it brings.

Study questions
- Chapter 10 tells us that we sometimes squander contentment because we focus on the wrong things. What nagging problems or minor details draw you away from feeling contented?
- Describe a moment in your life when you felt true contentment.
- Why do we find it so difficult to live in a contented way on a daily basis?

- What current situations do you have in your life that need a new approach, a response in love, instead of frustration and anger?
- What do you want Christ to do for you?

A step you might take in the week ahead to practice contentment more consistently. (Individual to supply)

Tell Me Your Story

I would love to hear about your journey and how God is working in your life. E-mail me at judy@judychristie.com. Remember: God created you for wonderful things. Enjoy today!

GOODBYE, MURPHY'S LAW